The Gainsharing Design Manual

The Gainsharing
Design Manual

Joseph H. Boyett, Ph.D.
and
Jimmie T. Boyett

ASJA Press
New York Lincoln Shanghai

The Gainsharing Design Manual

ASJA Press
an imprint of iUniverse, Inc.

For information address:
iUniverse, Inc.
2021 Pine Lake Road, Suite 100
Lincoln, NE 68512
www.iuniverse.com

ISBN: 0-595-32408-8

Printed in the United States of America

Contents

Introduction

Although there has been a tremendous increase in interest in gainsharing over the last few years, gainsharing itself is not new. It has been used successfully in the United States at least since the 1930s. Joseph Scanlon, a cost accountant and union official at the Empire Steel and Tin Plate Company in Mansfield, Ohio, developed the original concept. Faced with a company on the brink of bankruptcy, Scanlon persuaded company management and the union to cooperate in an effort to involve employees in generating ideas for improving productivity. Although there was no formal bonus system under the initial Empire plan, experience at Empire led to the application of union/management cooperative efforts at other companies and eventually to the addition of a bonus system to encourage employees to find ways to improve productivity.

In brief, gainsharing programs involve groups of employees in improving performance through better use of labor, capital, materials, and energy. In return for their efforts, the company shares part of the resultant savings from performance gains with employees in the form of a cash bonus, the amount of which is calculated according to some predetermined formula. It is important to note that under gainsharing programs, employees earn bonuses based upon group performance rather than individual performance and that employees are involved in finding ways to improve performance and make gains. Thus, gainsharing includes both a program for involving employees and a formula for calculating gains. The involvement system and formula are both vital to the success and longevity of the program.

Gainsharing Principles

Gainsharing is as much a philosophy of management as it is an incentive program. The following principles are vital to its success:

- *Open-Book Management*—A commitment on the part of management to share information, including financial information about the business, with employees; to be accessible to employees; and to educate employees about the business.

- *Employee Involvement*—A commitment on the part of management to teams, participative management, flat organizations, training, job enlargement, organizational learning and a willingness to listen to and act upon employee suggestions.

- *Equity*—A commitment to being accountable for and balancing the interest of all stakeholders including customers, investors, and employees; to honesty; and to the equitable sharing of financial rewards that flow from employee efforts and creativity.

If you do not share and/or the top leadership is not supportive of these principles, then you should NOT attempt to implement gainsharing.

Results from Gainsharing

What kinds of productivity, quality, and financial results might you expect from gainsharing? Here are findings reported in several of the many studies that have been conducted to assess the impact of gainsharing on company operating and financial performance over the last 25 years.

- A 1981 U. S. General Accounting Office survey of 24 firms with gainsharing plans found that companies with less than $100 million per year in sales had average savings of 17.3 percent per year from quality and productivity improvements. Companies with annual sales over $110 million had average savings of 16.4 percent. Over eighty percent of the gainsharing companies reported improvements in labor-management relations; over 47 percent reported a reduction in employee grievances; and over 36 percent reported a reduction in absenteeism and turnover. (See *Productivity Sharing Programs: Can They Contribute to Productivity Improvement?* GAO/AFMD-81-22, March 3, 1981)

- In a 1984 study of 33 gainsharing programs, 80 percent of the surveyed firms reported measurable improvements in productivity, cost savings, and/or quality with many reporting gains of 20 percent to 30 percent. Three-quarters of the surveyed firms reported additional improvements in employee satisfaction and morale and significant reductions in grievances. (See R. J. Bullock, *Gainsharing—A Successful Track Record*, World of Work Report, 9, 1984.)

- A large study conducted by the American Compensation Association between 1989 and 1994 found that companies with gainsharing had average savings of $2,410 per employee per year from productivity and quality improvements. After deducting program costs and bonus payments, these companies reported an average return of 222 percent per year on every dollar expended on their gainsharing programs. (See Jerry L. McAdams and Elizabeth J. Hawk. *Organizational Performance & Rewards: 663 Experiences in Making the Link*, American Compensation Association and Martiz Inc., 1994.)

- In a 1994 survey of 110 plants in Michigan, Ohio, Indiana, Wisconsin, and Minnesota with gainsharing programs, 36 percent of the plant managers reported productivity gains of 18 to 23 percent after installing gainsharing. Thirty-eight percent reported gains of 10 percent to 18 percent. Ten percent reported gains of less than 10 percent. (See *Crain's Chicago Business*, April 25-May 5, 1994, p.1)

- In a 1996 survey of 269 organizations with gainsharing plans...

  o 63 percent of respondents rated their gainsharing plan as successful or very successful;

  o Over 70 percent of respondents said gainsharing had resulted in improvements in productivity;

  o Over half said gainsharing had a positive impact on product quality;

  o Two-thirds said gainsharing led to lower production costs; and

  o Nearly 90 percent said employee suggestions generated by their gainsharing program had led to either major or minor improvements in production processes. (See Kenneth Mericle and Dong-One Kim. *Gainsharing and Goalsharing: Aligning Pay and Strategic Goals* Westport, Conneticut: Praeger, 2004, pp. 1-2.)

- In 2002, researchers from Loyola University and New Mexico State University compared the performance of six retail stores that had implemented trial gainsharing plans with the performance of a comparable group of six stores that had traditional forms of compensation. They found that...

  o Gainsharing stores had higher customer service scores than the non-gainsharing stores;

o   Employee turnover in gainsharing stores was 49 percent compared to 63 percent in non-gainsharing stores; and

o   Gainsharing stores had *significantly higher* sales performance to sales goals scores than non-gainsharing stores.

(See K. Dow Scott, Jane Floyd, Philip Benson, and James Bishop. "The Impact of the Scanlon Plan on Retail Score Performance," *World at Work Journal*, Vol. 11, No. 3, Third Quarter, 2002)

These kinds of results are impressive but we caution you that they are by no means guaranteed. Many companies have introduced gainsharing programs only to obtain poor or highly unsatisfactory results. For example, in 1989 the American Management Association surveyed 83 companies that had adopted gainsharing programs in the previous three years. One-third of the companies reported significant improvements in productivity accompanied by substantial reductions in waste, rejects and rework. However, two-thirds said their programs were flops and that any gains they achieved plateaued or declined after the first year or so. (Reported in Woodruff Imberman, "Gainsharing: A Lemon or Lemonade" *Business Horizons*, Vol. 39, Issue 1, Jan/Feb, 1996.)

The truth about gainsharing is that there are many documented success stories. It is also true that many gainsharing programs, perhaps half, survive less than five years with many losing their effectiveness after the first year or two. Gainsharing does work provided it is implemented at the right time, in the right way, with the support and commitment from managers and employees. We have designed this manual to help you avoid the pitfalls and design a gainsharing programs that has the greatest chance of success.

Gainsharing and Traditional Compensation

In his 1991 book, *Gainsharing* (Houston: Gulf Publishing, 1991) John Belcher identifies four significant problems with traditional compensation that are at least partially remedied by gainsharing.

Rewards not tied to performance—Belcher notes that under the type of compensation found in most companies today pay has little if any relation to performance for most employees. Most employees expect and usually get automatic pay increases year after year whether or not their performance improves. In the past companies simply passed the annual increase in labor costs along to customers in the form of price increases. Today, however, most companies are finding it increasingly difficult to raise prices on an annual basis. As a consequence, they are forced to absorb the extra labor costs, thus making less profit or denying their employees increases, and they suffer the declines in morale and defections that flat salaries inevitably bring. In contrast to traditional compensation, gainsharing ties a portion of employees' total compensation to performance improvement. Employees earn the increased compensation; they are not given it.

Inflexible wages and salaries—Belcher notes that in most companies compensation below the executive level largely becomes a fixed cost. There is a payroll that must be met—period. If times turn bad, managers have few options. They can cut out overtime, but their only real option to cut labor costs significantly is to layoff workers. Layoffs undermine morale and hurt employee commitment, but they are common in most industries. In contrast, gainsharing provides managers with another option. Under gainsharing, wages become much more flexible since a portion of every employee's total compensation, often a significant portion, is tied to group and/or company performance. In good times, the company and its workers prosper. In bad times, both suffer, but they suffer much less, than they might as a result of repeated layoffs.

Little reinforcement for performance—Belcher acknowledges that most companies pay lip service to rewarding good performance. Many companies say that they only provide "merit" increases. Supposedly, the high performers get the annual increases in pay while low performers get small increases or none at all. That is the way it is supposed to work. In reality, writes Belcher, true merit usually accounts for very little of the "merit" increase. Cost of living, the individual's position in the salary range, budget constraints, and a host of other factors are much more important in determining the amount of increase any person receives. Even when merit is a factor in determining the amount of increases, it makes little difference since the range from high to low is often very small, a few percentage points at most. On the other hand, gainsharing offers the possibility of substantial rewards for superior performance. Gainsharing bonuses may run well in excess of ten percent of base pay, and some companies such a Lincoln Electric in Cleveland, Ohio, have repeatedly paid bonuses of 100 percent of base pay.

Two-class pay culture—Finally Belcher notes that traditional compensation schemes often create a two-class pay culture. Salaried employees are treated as trustworthy and reliable. They get special privileges and better benefits. Hourly workers are told that they are the company's most important assets, but supervisors constantly watch them. They are forced to clock in and clock out to prove they are not cheating the company. If they are late, they are penalized. If they are early, they are looked upon with suspicion. By itself, gainsharing does not wipe out class differences between salaried and hourly workers, but it does level the playing field. Under gainsharing, hourly workers are rewarded for their participation and input in one of the best possible ways. They are compensated for it. Under the best gainsharing plans, salaried and hourly become financial partners. Everyone climbs into the same money boat.

Gainsharing versus Other Incentives

Companies usually adopt gainsharing for two primary reasons: (1) to hold the line on base pay increases, and (2) to make a portion of each employee's pay variable and tied to performance. Here is how gainsharing compares to several other pay-for-performance systems in respect to these objectives.

Gainsharing versus Individual Incentives

Individual incentives have been used for a long time, particularly in manufacturing settings. Obviously, such incentives tie pay directly to performance, and at least initially, they result in increased productivity. As long as good individual measures of performance can be maintained and there is no need for teamwork or cooperation between employees on the job, individual incentives can work. However, companies have found that, over time, individual incentives become increasingly more difficult and costly to administer, since base rate standards must be restudied and adjusted to keep them in line with changes in methods and technology. When such adjustments are made, they often result in employee complaints and/or intentional efforts by employees to restrict output to avoid a rate change. If adjustments are not made or if they are inaccurate, pay can lose its relationship to performance and inequities can develop.

Beyond the problem of administering individual incentives, most companies find that such incentives become inappropriate and even harmful as the nature of the work changes. Individual incentives encourage employees to focus on their own output without regard to the output of their plant, department, or unit. Under individual incentives, there is no inducement for employees to cooperate, work as a team, help each other, or place the interests of their company, plant, division, or unit over their own personal interest. As long as people work independently, teamwork and cooperation may not be so important. However, what happens when jobs become highly automated and servicing the new high-speed technology requires a group effort?

For many companies, gainsharing is an attractive alternative to individual incentives because it overcomes both of these problems. First, since measurements used in gainsharing are usually based on group performance, companies do not have to set and constantly update standards, thus avoiding most of the administrative costs associated with individual incentives. Second, gainsharing is based upon group rather than on individual performance. Gainsharing plans thus encourage teamwork, cooperation, and a long-term interest in achieving group goals.

Gainsharing versus Profit-Sharing or Lump-Sum Bonuses

Like gainsharing, profit-sharing plans and performance-based lump-sum bonuses rely upon macro-level measurements and are based upon group performance. Thus, profit-sharing and lump-sum bonuses have the same advantages over individual incentives as gainsharing. However, profit-sharing and lump-sum bonuses differ from gainsharing in some important ways. First, they usually make payouts only once or twice per year, and in the case of profit-sharing, part or all of the payment might be deferred into a retirement plan. In contrast, most gainsharing plans pay out monthly or quarterly. This difference in frequency of payment is important since most research has shown that an incentive is more powerful in stimulating performance if it occurs close to the time of the behavior.

A second problem with profit-sharing is that bonuses are tied to company profits, not employee performance. Thus, employees might perform exceptionally well but receive no bonus because the company was not profitable due to pricing policies, economic conditions, management decisions to write off losses, or any number of other factors over which employees have no control. Likewise, employees can receive a profit-sharing bonus even when there has been no productivity or performance gain. Under gainsharing, bonus payments are more closely tied to actual employee performance, particularly if the gainsharing formula is based upon physical rather than on financial measurements. This means that in some cases, employees can earn bonuses even when the company is not profitable. Over the long term, gainsharing should contribute to profitability, but gainsharing is usually not dependent upon profitability. As a result, employees have more control over their own destiny under gainsharing. At the same time, they are prevented from reaping benefits from results over which they had no direct control.

Gainsharing versus Skill-Based Pay and Pay-for-Competencies

Under skill-based pay, base pay or pay progression is tied to job knowledge or underlying competencies. The more jobs an employee can perform, the greater his or her depth of knowledge in a specialty, or the greater number of competencies he or she possesses, the higher his/her base pay is, regardless of whether he/she actually performs the jobs. Skill-based pay indirectly effects performance, since it encourages a more flexible workforce, thus reducing labor costs. Yet these systems do not tie pay directly to performance, which limits the widespread application of skill-based pay or pay-for-competencies. However, skill-based pay/competencies can be an important application if installed as an adjunct to gainsharing. (See Boyett & Conn, *Maximum Performance Management* (Glenbridge, 1988) for a discussion of the role for skill-based pay and how it can be used to offset a weakness in gainsharing plans.)

Gainsharing versus Small Group Incentives

Small group incentives have many of the same advantages as gainsharing. They are based upon macro measures of group performance, they tie pay directly to performance, and they can be paid out frequently. Yet, small group incentives have a severe disadvantage compared to gainsharing in that they can result in significant pay discrepancies from group to group and can encourage unhealthy inter-group rivalry. In contrast, gainsharing plans normally can be constructed so that such destructive competition is minimized or avoided altogether. In addition, the company's industrial engineer without employee participation generally designs small group incentives. As a result, they fail to create a partnership between employees and the company like gainsharing does.

Gainsharing versus Goalsharing

Gainsharing and goalsharing are quite similar. Both are group incentives and both award employees for meeting some pre-established targets. The key difference between gainsharing and goalsharing has to do with the types of measures that are used. Traditionally gainsharing plans reward employees for cost containment and/or productivity improvement and are self-funded from the cost savings. Goalsharing plans reward employees for meeting a broad range of specific goals such as job performance, quality, customer service and so on which may or may not be directly related to short-term, bottom-line, financial performance. Goalsharing plans must be funded from the value-added as a result of obtainment of the performance goals. Some compensation specialists argue that gainsharing should be used when your overall goal is cost containment. Goalsharing should be used when you wish to emphasize non-financial goals and/or you need to revitalize a gainsharing program that has grown stale because most of the cost savings have been achieved. Later when we discuss gainsharing formulas, we will illustrate goalsharing formulas also.

The Advantages of Gainsharing

To reiterate, gainsharing has these distinct advantages over other pay-for-performance options:

- It is based upon group, not individual performance;
- It encourages teamwork and cooperation;
- It is based on macro measures and thus is easy to administer;
- It results in payouts relatively close in time to performance;
- It is based upon factors that can be controlled by the group;
- It rarely encourages destructive competition between groups; and
- It promotes an employee/company partnership for improvement.

The Importance of Employee Involvement

Two factors are critical to the success of any gainsharing plan: (1) a provision for some type of structured employee involvement and (2) a formula for calculating gains. Both are equally important, although more attention is often given to developing the gainsharing formula than to creating a structured system for employee development and implementation of improvement ideas. Gainsharing programs fail as much as 40 percent of the time when there is just a formula and no structured system for involving employees. For this reason, we urge you to include a workable involvement system with a continuing structure when you implement gainsharing.

The types of involvement systems that will work with gainsharing include any structured method for providing feedback to employees on performance and for allowing employees to identify and solve problems. Under one of the oldest gainsharing programs, the Scanlon Plan, the involvement system uses production committees at the work-group level composed of managers, supervisors, and employees. These committees are responsible for soliciting, evaluating, and implementing employee suggestions. In addition, there typically is a plant-wide screening committee that receives and acts upon suggestions that the work-group level committees cannot implement by themselves.

We prefer using work-group teams as the basis for employee involvement. These teams follow the existing organizational hierarchy with the manager or supervisor serving as the team leader. All employees participate as members of the team on a non-voluntary basis. These teams communicate information about the gainsharing program and about performance on a regular basis. They also identify opportunities for performance gains, and they design and implement solutions. Cross-sectional and cross-functional problems identified by the work groups are assigned to problem-solving task forces or cross-functional problem-solving teams composed of managers, supervisors, and employees from all the work groups that could affect the specific performance problem under discussion. We explain more about this involvement system later in this manual.

Is Gainsharing Right for You?

There are many possible reasons for considering gainsharing, and when properly implemented, gainsharing can benefit many companies. Based upon our description of gainsharing so far, you might be considering gainsharing as an option. Obviously, we think gainsharing has much to offer, but it is not right for every company. Answer the questions in Exhibit I-1 to determine if gainsharing is right for you.

Exhibit I-1
Is Gainsharing Right for You?

	Question	Yes	No
1.	Does the organization in which you intend to implement gainsharing have fewer than 500 employees? [Note: Gainsharing can work with groups of up to 2,000, but is most successful when the participating group is smaller. There is some evidence that gainsharing is most successful with groups of 150 to 200.]		
2.	Is the culture of the organization egalitarian and participative? Do managers emphasize commitment over control? Is there widespread acceptance and commitment to the philosophy of gainsharing that we outlined earlier—Open book management, participation, and equity?		
3.	Do you have in place or are you willing to develop management systems that support open communication / sharing of financial and operating information with employees?		
4.	Is there a strong and compelling need for the organization to improve performance that justifies the kind of extensive change in workplace practices the gainsharing entails? Can you easily justify the sacrifices people will have to make in order to implement gainsharing?		
5.	Are at least 75 percent of senior managers at the site willing to support the implementation of gainsharing publicly and privately? Are they willing and able to commit financial and other resources under their control to the success of the gainsharing effort?		
6.	Is there at least one true champion of gainsharing at the site whose opinion is respected by other managers and employees and who is willing to use his/her influence and control over key resources (money, people, technology, etc.) to support gainsharing?		

	Question	Yes	No
7.	Is there at least one true champion of gainsharing at the corporate level whose opinion is respected by other managers and employees and who is willing to use his/her influence and control over key resources (money, people, technology, etc.) to support gainsharing?		
8.	Is there at least one person with experience or formal training in gainsharing on site who can be designated as the full-time gainsharing coordinator (½ time for sites with fewer than 200 employees) during a six-month to one-year implementation? If yes, who is that person? Name:_____		
9.	Are the following functional areas/departments considered to be effective, efficient, flexible, and trusted by employees, and are they able to communicate effectively with employees: [Note: Each of these will be called upon to support gainsharing.]		
	Engineering		
	Maintenance		
	Purchasing		
	Scheduling		
	Quality Assurance		
	Personnel/Human Resources		
	Accounting		
10.	Do the technology and work processes at the location to be covered by gainsharing require/benefit from employee information sharing, teamwork, and cooperation?		

	Question	Yes	No
11.	Is accurate financial information (data on revenues, costs, etc.) available for the site for at least three to five years?		
12.	Is accurate operating data (productivity, quality, customer satisfaction, throughput time, and so on) available for the site for at least the last three to five years?		
13.	If productivity improved as a result of gainsharing, is there sufficient market for the increased product and/or work that could be shifted to the site to absorb the increased capacity?		
14.	Are the product/service lines relatively stable? [Note: It is probably not wise to install gainsharing at the same time you are undergoing a major change in product/service lines.]		
15.	Is the site free from significant seasonal fluctuations in demand? [Note: If the organization is subject to seasonal fluctuations, that reality must be accounted for in the design of the gainsharing formula and establishment of gainsharing targets.]		
16.	Are major capital investments planned for the site in the near future that might significantly change the labor input required to produce the product or service?		
17.	Is employee job satisfaction at the site relatively high?		
18.	Do employees trust site managers?		
19.	Are labor/management relations at the site positive?		
20.	If there is a union, is the union supportive or at least neutral when it comes to gainsharing?		

HOW TO EVALUATE YOUR ANSWERS:

If your management team's answers to all of the above questions were yes, then you most likely have in place or can develop the management practices and systems necessary for a successful gainsharing program. If you answered no to one or more of these questions or were unsure about your answers, then you must give special consideration to the issues raised in those questions to which you gave "no" or unsure answers during the design phase of gainsharing so that you can correct any problems before the plan is installed.

Unions and Gainsharing

Most unions today are either neutral toward gainsharing or mildly in favor of it. Union support is normally the result of the belief, on the part of union leadership, that gainsharing will accomplish the following:

- Provide increased recognition for employee performance;

- Increase job security for union members by making the company more successful;

- Allow employees to have more control over the way they do their jobs;

- Provide employees with the opportunity to earn bonuses; and

- Allow employees to have an impact on the company.

Union opposition normally stems from one or more of the following:

- Suspicion that management is trying to substitute gainsharing for base wage increases;

- Fear that the company management can't be trusted and as a result will manipulate bonus calculations, change the rules of the game to avoid making bonus payments, or layoff workers if productivity improves;

- Concern that peer pressure will increase to intolerable levels once gainsharing is implemented;

- Fear that employees will not be able to earn bonuses because the formula includes items out of workers' control; and/or

- Fear that the employee involvement portion of gainsharing is simply an attempt by management to undermine the union and create a sham union.

Gainsharing consultants Timothy L. Ross and Ruth Ann Ross suggested that you are most likely to obtain union cooperation if you do the following:

- Reassure union leaders that productivity gains will not lead to layoffs;

- Involve the union in the gainsharing design process;

- Keep the gainsharing plan out of contract negotiations that are usually adversarial in nature (Gainsharing should be kept separate from wage negotiations.);

- Open the books and share information (You are going to have to do this with employees anyway if you want gainsharing to be successful.);

- Be open and frank about the advantages and disadvantages of gainsharing for both the company and employees;

- Include union representatives on any fact-finding teams you might send to other union and non-union gainsharing companies;

- Respond to union concerns honestly and quickly;

- Consider creating a joint union/management committee to oversee the implementation and administration of gainsharing; and

Whatever you do, do not use gainsharing against the union.

[See Timothy L. Ross and Ruth Ann Ross, "Gainsharing and Unions: Current Trends," in Brian Graham-Moore and Timothy L. Ross. *Gainsharing: Plans for Improving Performance*, Washington, D.C.: Bureau of National Affairs, 1990, Pp. 200-213.]

20 Keys to Gainsharing Success

Extensive research has been conducted over the last 30 years on the success of gainsharing. Here are twenty of the most important keys to success based upon the experiences of Boyett & Associates and other gainsharing consultants with hundreds of gainsharing plans.

1. Build a business case for gainsharing. Align the program and rewards with the business strategy. How will gainsharing support your business objectives?

2. Be cautious about implementing gainsharing in a capital-intensive organization. Gainsharing has been shown to be most successful in labor-intensive

organizations where employees can significantly influence performance outcomes thorough their ideas and actions.

3. Do not implement gainsharing during times of financial crisis or if the business does not have the funds to invest in program administration and employee development and training.

4. Use outside consultants sparingly. They can be a useful resource but do not rely upon them too heavily. Managers and employees must design the gainsharing plan themselves in order to develop a sense of ownership of the plan and to acquire the skills to be able to maintain and revise the plan over time.

5. Do not attempt to design the plan in isolation. Gainsharing plans designed by outside consultants or a single or small group of managers without employee and/or union input are doomed to failure.

6. Prepare to spend from six to nine months designing the gainsharing plan. It takes that amount of time to work through all of the issues and to gain commitment to the plan. Plans that are designed in haste quickly fail.

7. If there is a union, involve the union early on in the gainsharing design process. You must gain union support or at least acquiescence to gainsharing or your plan cannot succeed.

8. Involve employees in the decision to undertake gainsharing and in the design process. Consider having employees vote on the plan and do not implement the plan unless 80 percent of employees approve.

9. Keep the gainsharing participant group relatively small. The number of participants covered by a single gainsharing plan should be less than 500 and preferably less than 200.

10. Keep the plan simple and easy to understand. Ensure that the formula contains only items that are controllable by plan participants.

11. Make sure that gainsharing targets are reasonable and justifiable given historical trends and competitive requirements and that they are seen as fair and reasonable by employees and managers alike.

12. Do not implement gainsharing if the potential for gains is unlikely to produce average bonus payments of $100 per month per employee. Ideally, employees should have the potential to earn average bonuses of $200 per month or more. Research suggests that it takes bonuses, or at least the

potential for bonuses, of $100 per month to get employees' attention and $200 per month to get them excited.

13. Calculate and pay gainsharing bonuses monthly or weekly rather than quarterly or annually. Employees will see a greater connection between their efforts and gainsharing bonuses if the bonuses are paid close to the time of the performance that led to the gain.

14. Do not attempt to implement gainsharing without strong support from the senior executives of the organization and the majority of managers and supervisors. The senior manager of the organization implementing gainsharing should be prepared to state his/her commitment to the philosophy of gainsharing and the organization's gainsharing plan both verbally and in writing prior to the implementation of the plan.

15. Make sure a structured system of employee involvement such as employee teams or a suggestion system is in place and operational BEFORE the start of gainsharing and that employees and managers are fully trained in the operation of the system.

16. Make sure employees understand the drivers of the gainsharing formula and how they can affect the potential for gains. There should be a direct "line-of-sight" between employee behavior and gainsharing results.

17. Invest heavily in employee training and re-training to ensure that employees understand the gainsharing plan and have the problem-solving and other skills necessary to find ways to make gains happen.

18. Make extensive use of banners, meetings, bulletin boards, newsletters and other communication devices to keep employees informed about the status of the gainsharing program during the design process and once the program is implemented. Communicate, communicate, communicate, communicate, communicate, communicate, communicate, communicate...then communicate some more.

19. Implement the gainsharing plan when business conditions are good and there is the potential to realize early gains.

20. Conduct regularly scheduled formal reviews of the gainsharing plan (at least annually) to make sure the plan is working for employees, the company and other stakeholders. Revise the plan as necessary.

1

Getting Started

Awareness Raising and the Feasibility Study

You should have a fair idea about the appropriateness of gainsharing in your company by now. Assuming that you have chosen to proceed, your next step is to design your gainsharing program. Fortunately, there is much accumulated wisdom about the design and implementation processes from those who have installed gainsharing over the last sixty years. They advise that you take the following steps to design your program:

STEP 1: Getting started

> *Awareness raising*

> *Feasibility study*

> *The Feasibility report*

STEP 2: Developing the gainsharing incentive plan

> *Gainsharing task force membership*

> *Implementation timeline*

> *Gainsharing objectives*

> *Participant group*

> *Eligibility requirements*

> *Allocation basis*

Performance period

Holdback provision

Sunset provision

Adjustment provision

Payback provision

Bonus ceiling

Sharing ratio

Administrative details

STEP 3: Designing the Gainsharing Formula

Choosing from standard formulas—Scanlon, Rucker, Improshare

Designing a custom formula

Setting the gainsharing target/baseline

STEP 4: Creating the Involvement System

Involvement system

Involvement system training

STEP 5: Implementing, evaluating and maintaining your gainsharing program

Implementation

Evaluation

We will examine each of these steps and where appropriate provide examples of model gainsharing plans, showing how the issue may be addressed.

In this chapter, we address awareness raising and the feasibility study.

Awareness Raising

The implementation of gainsharing results in significant changes for most companies. Not only are compensation practices changed, but the entire management culture changes as well. Top-level management commitment is essential to the successful accomplishment of this degree of change. Therefore, the first step toward implementing gainsharing is to secure that top-level commitment through the use of information and awareness-raising programs. Here are some things to do:

1. Compile a library of books and articles on gainsharing and circulate these among senior managers. The history of gainsharing is extensively documented, and you should have little problem locating materials at your local library and/or over the Internet. If you do have trouble, contact the Scanlon Leadership Network.

    ### Scanlon Leadership Network

    2875 Northwind Drive, Suite 121, East Lansing, MI 48823, (517) 332-8927 or http://www.scanlonleader.org.

    They can provide numerous publications on gainsharing and can supply you with resources, educational materials, best practices and access to web sites of members of the Scanlon Leadership Network who have implemented Scanlon-type gainsharing plans. In addition, we have included a list of suggested readings at the end of this manual that you may find helpful.

2. Based upon the information you have collected, prepare short summaries describing gainsharing, and arrange briefings for key managers.

3. As you review the case studies you collected and other documentation, you will identify companies that have adopted gainsharing. Most of these companies are very willing to share their experiences with you and, if you wish, to arrange for some of your key managers to visit them and learn about gainsharing firsthand.

Your objective in this step is to secure sufficient top-level interest in gainsharing to commit resources (people, time, money) to a feasibility study.

Feasibility Study

We strongly recommend that you conduct a feasibility study before proceeding with gainsharing. There are too many issues associated with gainsharing and too great a risk of failure if the program is implemented poorly to ignore the need for a beginning assessment.

Gainsharing Task Force Membership—Feasibility Study

To conduct the feasibility study, we suggest that top-level management appoint a gainsharing task force comprised of the following:

- The president of the company or, at a minimum, a senior executive,

- The plant manager or location manager of the site at which gainsharing will first be installed,

- The company comptroller or financial manager,

- The personnel or human resources manager, and

- Several other key managers, such as the quality control manager or industrial engineering manager.

CAUTIONARY NOTE: We have tried to provide you with a practical guide to gainsharing design in this manual, but no manual can begin to answer all of the questions that may arise as you design your gainsharing plan. Therefore, we suggest that you hire a gainsharing consultant to help you with the feasibility study and subsequent design, development, and installation of gainsharing. We make this recommendation because you can save a lot of time and expense by having the advice of someone who has been through this process before. In addition, you will need the objectivity an outsider can bring to the process. About 90 percent of the gainsharing programs that have been installed successfully have had the benefit of consulting assistance. Additionally, gainsharing deals with sensitive pay issues and impacts labor relations. Therefore, we recommend that you have all aspects of your plan, its design and implementation reviewed by a competent attorney and qualified financial advisor before installation.

Content of the Feasibility Study

The feasibility study focuses on five areas of concern:

1. *Strategic direction.*

Objective: To determine how gainsharing might support implementation of the organization's strategic plan.

Action: Conduct interviews with senior management about strategic issues and concerns.

2. *Potential for gains.*

Objective: To identify any critical areas of performance that should be emphasized by any gainsharing formula and the potential for improvement in these areas.

Action: Interview senior managers to identify critical measures of performance and compile data on current performance levels, targets and potential for improvement.

3. *Top management attitudes.*

Objective: To determine the attitudes of top management and other key employees concerning their support for the gainsharing principles (open book management, employee involvement, and equity) and their assessment of the appropriateness of gainsharing to the organization.

Action: Conduct interviews with top management and other key employees concerning their willingness to support participative management and gainsharing.

4. *Organizational dependencies.*

Objective: To determine if a group-based incentive is appropriate for the organization, given existing operating procedures and process flows.

Action: Review current operating procedures and process flows. Look for major inputs and outputs and the interdependence of functions in order to determine how critical teamwork and cooperation between functions are for performance.

5. *Organizational climate*

Objective: To determine if existing management-employee relations and management practices support the teamwork, cooperation, and employee involvement that will be necessary to support gainsharing.

Action: Interview middle management, supervisors and a sample of employees to determine the following:

- The level of knowledge about and reaction to gainsharing;

- Knowledge of the company's strategic direction and departmental/unit mission;

- The nature of and reaction to organizational changes that have occurred in the last few years, such as changes in management, work methods, technology, human resource management practices, and so on (Determine whether the changes were successful and how managers, supervisors, and employees received them.);

- The existence and quality of top-down communication;

- The existence and quality of communication across functions and shifts;

- The use of supervisor and employee meetings and what happens in these meetings;

- Whether operational goals and objectives exist at every level (Are they understood and viewed as fair and reasonable?);

- The existence of measurements and feedback systems;

- The use of social reinforcement;

- The use of performance appraisals (Do they exist? How are they done? How helpful are they?);

- Decision-making/problem-solving styles and existence of and reaction to any employee involvement programs;

- The existence of group and/or incentive plans (Would they support or conflict with gainsharing?);

- The ideas of managers, supervisors, and employees concerning key areas for focus under gainsharing (Also, their assessment of the potential for gains through changes in employee behavior.); and

- The state of employee job satisfaction in term of morale, trust, and overall management/employee relations.

These interviews should be conducted one-on-one and in private. The interviewees must be assured of the confidentiality of their answers.

The Feasibility Report

Once the feasibility study is completed, a formal report outlining findings, conclusions, and recommendations should be prepared. The report should include the following types of information.

- *Key findings from the feasibility study.* Key findings should be presented for all the interview areas. This section of the report should be written whether or not gainsharing is found to be feasible. Even if you determine that gainsharing is not right for your company, you may be able to identify significant opportunities for improvement in management practices as a result of these interviews. Such findings should not be lost simply because gainsharing is not appropriate. In fact, it might be possible to correct some management problems identified during the feasibility study and, as a result, reconsider gainsharing at a later date.

- *Recommendations.* The gainsharing task force should make a recommendation either to proceed with the design and development step or to discontinue the effort. If a decision is made to proceed, the task force should draw up an implementation plan and cost estimates. These recommendations must then be submitted to senior management for approval.

- *Preliminary recommendations about the formula.* If gainsharing is considered to be feasible, the report should outline preliminary recommendations about a gainsharing calculation or formula. No specific customized formula need be proposed at this time, but the report should at least address the major factors that will be included in such a formula once it is developed.

- *Involvement issues.* If gainsharing is considered feasible, the involvement portion of the feasibility report must address how employees will be provided an opportunity to generate and implement ideas for performance improvement and how information about the gainsharing program and performance will be shared with employees. If changes are required, they should be identified and a plan presented to the gainsharing task force for implementing them. This plan might call for training of managers and supervisors in management techniques, the design and implementation of new reporting and feedback systems, and so on. (See our discussion of employee involvement elsewhere in this manual.)

The reports should be structured around questions and issues like the following:

- *Strategic Direction*

How would gainsharing strengthen the organization's planned strategic direction?

- *Top Management Attitude*

What is the attitude of top management at your location toward participative management and gainsharing?

- *Potential for Gains*

Which area(s) of performance should be the focus of the gainsharing effort?

What is the potential for improvement in these areas?

What would happen if the organization became twice as productive as it is now? Do you have or can you obtain the volume of business to support a doubling of productivity and not have to resort to layoffs?

- Organizational dependencies

Are performance gains dependent upon cooperation and teamwork? If so, how?

- *Organizational Climate*

Exhibit 1.1 lists several "areas of concern" dealing with management/employee relations and the general organizational climate. In the space provided indicate the strengths and weaknesses of the organization where gainsharing is being considered in respect to each area of concern. Also, indicate any action that the Gainsharing Task Force feels is necessary to correct any weakness or capitalize on a strength before or during gainsharing implementation.

Exhibit 1.1
Assessment of Organizational Climate

Areas of Concern	Strength/Positive	Weakness/Negative	Required Action
Business Knowledge: Employee knowledge of company strategic direction and department or unit mission.			
Reaction to Change: How employees have reacted to organizational change that has occurred in the last few years, such as changes in management, work methods, technology, etc.?			
Top-Down Communication: What mechanisms do senior executives of the organization use to communicate with lower level managers, supervisors and employees? What is the quality of this communication?			
Cross Functional/ Cross Shift Communication: The quality of communication across functions and shifts.			
Team/Employee Meetings: The conduct of regular meetings with employees/team members? What happens in these meetings? Can these meetings support problem solving and communication in a gainsharing program?			
Goal Setting: Do operational and/or financial goals and objectives exist at every level? Are they understood? How are they set? Are they viewed as fair and reasonable?			

Areas of Concern	Strength/Positive	Weakness/Negative	Required Action
Measurement and Feedback Systems: Do objective and reliable measurement systems exist at all levels to provide employees and managers regular feedback on performance against goals and objectives?			
Recognition and Reinforcement: Is social reinforcement used to recognize and reward employee and team performance? How effective are existing recognition systems?			
Performance Assessment: Are individual performance appraisals conducted? How are they conducted? How frequently are they conducted? How helpful are they?			
Decision-Making Problem Solving: How are decisions made? How involved are lower level employees in problem solving? Is there a formal suggestion system or employee involvement system? What is the reaction of executives, managers, and supervisors to employee involvement or participative management?			
Incentive Systems: Does this organization currently have individual, group or management incentive programs? What are they? Are they effective? Are they consistent with gainsharing?			

Areas of Concern	Strength/Positive	Weakness/Negative	Required Action
Ideas for Improvement: What are manager, supervisor, and employee evaluations of key areas for focus under gainsharing? What is the potential for gains through changes in employee behavior?			
Job Satisfaction: What is the current state of employee morale, trust, and overall state of management/employee relations?			
Union/Management Relations: Is there a union? If so, what is the status of union and management relations? Does the union support gainsharing? Will the union participate in the gainsharing design? Why or why not?			

- *Recommendation of the Task Force*

Based on the answers to the questions above, what is the recommendation of the gainsharing task force?

A. Gainsharing should be implemented immediately.

    If the answer is **YES**, proceed to the next part of this manual to begin designing the gainsharing program.

B. Implementation of gainsharing should be postponed until the following actions have been taken. (Include a list of actions.)

    If the recommendation is to postpone implementation, implement the actions to correct any problems and then revisit the feasibility study. We do not recommend that you proceed with gainsharing until there is a consensus among the Gainsharing Task Force membership and senior management that gainsharing is desirable for the organization and has a good chance of success.

2

Designing the Gainsharing Plan

Design of Operating and Administrative Procedures

Having obtained the feasibility study recommendations, the gainsharing task force can proceed with designing the gainsharing plan.

The work of the gainsharing task force should be organized around the preparation of a gainsharing design document, which will address all the major issues of implementation, operation, and on-going administration of the gainsharing program. The segments of the gainsharing design document are as follows:

Part 1: Operating and Administrative Provisions

      Section 1.1—The Gainsharing Task Force

      Section 1.2—Implementation Timeline

      Section 1.3—Objectives of the Gainsharing Program

      Section 1.4—Participant Group

      Section 1.5—Eligibility Requirements

      Section 1.6—Allocation basis

      Section 1.7—Performance period

      Section 1.8—Holdback provision

      Section 1.9—Sunset Provision

      Section 1.10—Adjustment Provision

The task force must make critical decisions about the gainsharing program in preparing each of these segments of the gainsharing design document. We will discuss the preparation of Part 1: Operating and Administrative Procedures in this chapter. We will cover the remaining parts in the chapters that follow.

Part 1:
Operating and Administrative Provisions

The *Operating and Administrative Provisions* portion of the Gainsharing Design Document deals with the following issues:

Section 1.1—The Gainsharing Task Force

Section 1.2—Implementation Timeline

Section 1.3—Objectives of the Gainsharing Program

Section 1.4—Participant Group

Section 1.5—Eligibility Requirements

Section 1.6—Allocation basis

Section 1.7—Performance period

Section 1.8—Holdback provision

Section 1.9—Sunset Provision

Section 1.10—Adjustment Provision

Section 1.11—Buyback Provision

Section 1.12—Bonus Ceiling

Section 1.13—Sharing Ratio

Section 1.14—Plan Administration

Section 1.1—The Gainsharing Task Force

Up to this point, the gainsharing task force has been composed of seven members:

- The president or a senior manager,

- The plant or location manager,

- The comptroller,

- The personnel or human resources manager, and

- Three other key managers.

Before the start of formula design, new members should be added to the task force. These additional members should include:

- Functional area managers,

- The union president or a union steward, if there is a union, and

- Employee representatives. (See the cautionary note on the next page.)

After adding these members, the task force should ideally consist of between twelve and eighteen members.

CAUTIONARY NOTE: Ideally, there should be employee representatives on the gainsharing task force. Their participation builds trust and sends the message that the company is interested in employee ideas and committed to building a true partnership. Unfortunately, due to some outdated labor laws, the courts and federal regulatory agencies may consider such employee participation illegal.

The issue involves the interpretation of Sec. 8 of the National Labor Relations Act. For that reason, we encourage you to obtain competent legal advice and opinions before including employees on the task force. The two most directly relevant rulings by the National Labor Relations Board are the *Electromation* case (309 NLRB No. 163, December 16,1992) and the *Crown Cork & Seal* case (334 NLRB No. 92, July 20, 2001). The *Electromation* case raised doubt about the legality of employee involvement. The *Crown Cork & Seal* case appears to allow employee involvement.

Whether you include employees on the task force or not, we encourage you to adopt an open-door policy concerning the task force. Allow anyone who wishes to do so to attend task force meetings as an observer. Encourage them to enter into discussions, make suggestions and ask questions concerning issues before the task force.

Using a Gainsharing Consultant

You may wish to employ a consultant experienced in the design of gainsharing plans to assist the design task force. Among other things the consultant can:

- Train task force members on gainsharing;

- Lead task force meetings;

- Offer expert advice and assistance on design issues,

- Provide a third party, "neutral" point of view in case of disagreements over design issues;

- Conduct research on issues raised by the task force;

- Assist with plan documentation;

- Perform "what if" calculations to test proposed gainsharing formulas;

- Conduct statistical analysis to assist the task force in establishing reasonable gainsharing targets;

- Assist the task force in preparing and giving presentations to management; and

- Assist the task force in employee communication.

If you wish, Boyett & Associates can assist you with all of the above. Please contact us at 770-667-9904 for details. In addition, the Scanlon Leadership Network (517-332-8927 or http://www.ScanlonLeader.org) maintains a list of consultants with experience in implementing the Scanlon gainsharing process.

Plant X Gainsharing Plan Documentation

Section 1.1—The Gainsharing Task Force

The following individuals served on the gainsharing task force and were primarily responsible for the design of our gainsharing plan. Our Gainsharing Task Force included representatives of management, the union, and employee representatives from all three shifts.

Proposed Task Force Members

NAME	TITLE
Roland Johnson	Comptroller
Marie Holt	Finishing Manager
Len Olsten	Maintenance Manager
Dianne Burch	Personnel Manager
Jim Carter	Plant Manager
Lynn Brown	Quality Control Manager
Paul Gregg	Supervisor, 1st shift
Jerry Williams	Union Steward

Employee Representatives

Craig Capshaw, 1st shift
Butch Carter, 3rd shift
Toby Dawson, 1st shift
Jo Legette, 2nd shift
Beverly Lewis, office support staff
Terry Swanson, 2nd shift
Len Tealman, 3rd shift

Section 1.2—Implementation Timeline

The implementation timeline is a project schedule or plan showing all the activities that must be completed before the introduction of gainsharing, including target dates for completion of these activities. The timeline should cover activities related both to formula development and approval, as well as to implementation of the involvement system.

A key to the timeline and success of gainsharing itself is the task force's decision about the targeted start date for gainsharing. Every effort should be made to pick a start date which assures that the volume of work activity will allow gains to be made, provided employees work harder and smarter. For example, if your workload is seasonal, the low volume periods should be avoided. The worst thing that can happen is to start gainsharing and then experience months during which employees are unable to earn gains in spite of their efforts. Though selection of an appropriate start date requires a certain amount of forecasting on the part of task force members, it is a very important decision.

When discussing various possible start dates, the task force should ensure that it is allowing sufficient time for completion of all required activities and approvals leading up to gainsharing. For example, corporate attorneys or other officials will most likely have to review any proposed formula before its acceptance. Time must be built into the schedule for this review process. Do not be surprised if the timeline that is finally developed stretches over six months or even a year.

The benefit of developing a detailed timeline early in the process is that task force members will have to be familiar with the entire development and implementation process to develop the timeline. As a result, they will have to acquire a thorough understanding of the sequence of events and their responsibilities.

Plant X Gainsharing Plan Documentation

Section 1.2—Implementation Timeline

Week Ending	Activity	Participants
XX/XX/XX	Selection of Gainsharing Task Force—Management Representatives	Plant Manager
XX/XX/XX	Hire consultant	Task force members
XX/XX/XX	Gainsharing Task Force training (1 day)	Consultant(s) Task force members
XX/XX/XX	Overview for employees (multiple 2-hour sessions)	All employees
XX/XX/XX	Employee Vote/Survey	All employees
XX/XX/XX	Election of Employee Representatives for Gainsharing Task Force	All employees
XX/XX/XX	Gainsharing Task Force Meeting—Plan Objectives	Consultant(s) Task force members

///
///

XX/XX/XX	Legal review of plan	Corporate lawyers
XX/XX/XX	Final senior management approval	Senior executives Task force members
XX/XX/XX	Kick off meeting	All employees
XX/XX/XX	Gainsharing Starts	

Section 1.3—Objectives of the Gainsharing Program

After establishing a timeline, the task force should turn its attention to drafting a statement outlining the objectives for the gainsharing program. Although these objectives might seem obvious—to improve productivity, pay bonuses, etc.—they are actually more complicated than they first appear. Ideally, gainsharing should satisfy multiple, and sometimes competing interests, including those of employees, managers, stockholders, and customers. One of these interests is to share the financial and other gains from increased work performance with employees. However, sharing gains is not the only, and perhaps not even the most important objective of gainsharing. Others might include some of the following:

- Providing more job security as a result of increased productivity;

- Increasing recognition for performance;

- Improving communication;

- Increasing employee involvement;

- Improving productivity;

- Improving quality;

- Increasing problem identification and problem solving;

- Improving teamwork and cooperation;

- Increasing organizational flexibility;

- Improving competitiveness;

- Improving sales and profits;

- Reducing costs;

- Providing an opportunity for increased earnings based upon performance;

- Reducing resistance to change;

- Promoting an attitude of continuous improvement;

- Meeting strategic goals and objectives; and

- Eliminating individual incentives.

When developing gainsharing objectives, the task force should consider all the relevant interests—those of managers, employees, stockholders, customers—and develop objectives that could be supported by all these groups. Additionally, the objectives should provide some direction concerning how they can be achieved. For example, instead of proposing the objective "to reduce costs," you may want to expand the wording to something like the following:

> *To reduce unit costs with particular emphasis on the cost of labor, raw materials, and machine parts so that we can be the low cost producer.*

Ideally the objectives should include objectives to improve financial and operating performance and objectives to improve moral, job satisfaction, teamwork, labor/management cooperation, and so on. The more specific you are in wording the gainsharing objectives the easier it will be to develop a gainsharing formula targeted to achieve those objectives. For example, if you include an objective such as "reducing unit costs," you will obviously end up including labor, raw materials, and other costs in your formula.

Plant X Gainsharing Plan Documentation

Section 1.3—Objectives of Our Gainsharing Plan

The gainsharing program for *Plant X* will attempt to meet the following objectives:

- To increase teamwork, cooperation and communication between departments and shifts, improve employee morale, encourage individual initiative, reduce resistance to change, encourage employees to be self-managed, and generally make the *Plant X* a better place to work.

- To maintain a safe work environment. The operation of the gainsharing program shall be consistent in all respects with *Plant X*'s corporate priority to invest in safety programs, safety equipment, and safe manufacturing processes. The safety of our employees is paramount. Working safely does not cost money—it saves money!

- To decrease cost per unit by increasing overall production by doing the following:

  o   Minimizing waste, scrap and reworks,

  o   Improving labor efficiency,

  o   Reducing machine downtime, and

  o   Improving overall performance of machinery and other equipment.

- To improve customer service and satisfaction. This objective is consistent with *Plant X*'s corporate priority for excellent customer service and its commitment to listen to, stay close to and satisfy our customers.

- To improve quality. This objective supports *Plant X*'s and corporate objectives to provide products that will meet or exceed the appropriate specifications and customer expectations.

- To provide all *Plant* X's employees with an opportunity for increased earnings through sustainable improvements in productivity, customer service, and quality. Gainsharing will provide employees a share of the day-to-day gains.

- To promote a true partnership environment in which managers and employees work together as a team, share financial and operating information, trust each other, and take pride in company performance. Such an environment should enable the plant to attract, motivate, and retain the best people.

Section 1.4—Participant Group

After preparing a statement of objectives, the task force must next decide who will be included in the gainsharing program. Again, this decision appears simple at first, but it rarely is. For example, the participant group may be any combination of the following:

- Only direct employees, or direct and indirect employees;

- Only full-time employees, or full-time and part-time employees;

- Only permanent employees, or permanent and temporary employees;

- Only hourly employees, or employees, managers, supervisors, and nonexempt employees.

Key to these decisions is the interdependence of the various groups and the determination as to who can contribute to possible gains. For example, if the work of some or all of the indirect employees will significantly affect the potential for gains, then indirects likely should be included. If you use a large number of temporaries and will require their commitment to achieve targeted gains, you should give serious consideration to including them in the participant group.

Often, managers already participate in some kind of bonus incentive plan that is tied to organizational performance. If your managers have an incentive plan and you choose to retain this management-only incentive, make sure it is consistent with the gainsharing program. However, if you include managers in the participant group for gainsharing, you should discontinue the management-only plan to avoid double dipping, i.e., receiving two bonuses for the same performance.

Group Size

In the process of determining who should be included in the participant group, you should take the size of the participant group into consideration. Experience with gainsharing programs suggests that the ideal size of a participant group is two hundred or fewer employees. Larger groups, particularly those of more than two thousand employees, are generally considered poor candidates for a single gainsharing program. The larger the participant group, the less likely it is that employees will see how their individual effort contributes significantly to group performance. If you determine that the participant group will be very large, you may want to consider subdividing the large group and creating multiple gainsharing programs.

CAUTIONARY NOTE. A study conducted in New Zealand sheds some light on the way group incentives like gainsharing can affect employee turnover rates. The study examined retention/turnover in 153 New Zealand firms that offered skill-based pay and gainsharing. The results showed that skill-based pay improved retention while gainsharing, at least in this study, had a negative impact on turnover in some companies. The positive effect of skill-based pay presumably results from employee perception that this incentive is evidence of a commitment on the part of the company to employee development.

Gainsharing, on the other hand, had a negative impact on turnover in large organizations—those with over 300 employees. The negative effect was even stronger for organizations with more than 700 employees. Presumably, the turnover resulted from "free-rider" effects that are felt more strongly in large organizations. Even worse, the study found that high performers were the ones most likely to leave. There was no such negative impact in organizations with fewer than 300 employees.

In short, this study suggests that pay-for-skill is a good retention strategy regardless of the size of the organization but that gainsharing should only be used in organizations of 300 or fewer employees. Otherwise, you risk losing your high performers.

See James P. Guthrie, "Alternative Pay Practices and Employee Turnover: An Organization Economics Perspective," *Group & Organization Management*, Volume 25, No.4, December 2000, pp. 419-439.

Plant X Gainsharing Plan Documentation

Section 1.4—Participant Group

All employees at *Plant X* can affect the cost, productivity, quality and customer satisfaction with our products and services. Therefore, all executives, managers, supervisors, salaried exempt, salaried nonexempt and hourly employees in the company will participate in the gainsharing program.

Only permanent, full- or part-time employees who meet eligibility requirements will participate. Temporary employees, such as those who might be employed by the plant during the summer, will participate in the gainsharing program only if they meet length of service and other eligibility requirements.

Section 1.5—Eligibility Requirements

Eligibility refers to the requirements, if any, that must be met by members of the participant group before they can receive bonus payments. For example, normally there is a provision that new hires must complete a specified number of days of employment before being eligible for gainsharing bonuses. Additionally, the task force must make decisions concerning the effect that unexcused absences, personal leave, sick leave, and so on will have on eligibility or on the basis for calculating bonus payments. As a general rule, employees should become eligible as soon as they can contribute to gains.

Plant X Gainsharing Plan Documentation

Section 1.5—Eligibility Requirements

A permanent, full- or part-time employee must have completed 90 days of employment (probationary period) to be eligible for the group incentive/gain-sharing payout.

Bonuses will be based on total earnings for the gainsharing accounting period. Employees are not paid for unexcused or excused-without-pay absences, personal leaves, and medical leaves, therefore these absences will reduce the dollar amount of bonus payout during a particular period for an individual who misses work for one of these reasons. Disability pay will not be included in earnings at any time.

Absences for which an employee is paid their normal pay, including death in his/her immediate or extended family, jury duty, holidays, military leave or vacation, in accordance with current company policy, will not affect the bonus payout. These earnings will be included as part of an employee's total earnings for the bonus calculations.

Earnings during the 90-day probationary period will not be included in gross income for the year for holdback payout calculations.

Employees on medical or personal leaves of absence and employees who are laid off after completing their initial 90-day period will become eligible immediately for gainsharing payout in proportion to their gross earnings during the financial accounting period during which they re-enter the plant's work force.

Section 1.6—Allocation Basis

The task force makes several decisions pertaining to the allocation of gainsharing bonuses. The decisions include the following:

- *The method of payment.* Bonuses can be paid as part of regular paychecks or in the form of a separate check. Separate checks maintain the distinction between the gainsharing bonus and base pay, thereby providing greater motivational impact. You may even want use a different color for bonus checks in order to set them apart from regular paychecks. For example, Beth Israel hospital used a bright purple check with the words "Thank You" written across it as their gainsharing bonus check.

- *The payout period.* The difference in time between the performance period and the actual issuance of checks depends greatly upon the efficiency of your accounting and payroll functions. It is preferable, for motivational reasons, to make payments as close as possible to the period of performance they cover, however, the task force needs to ensure that the payout period allows adequate time to issue checks.

- *Payout calculation.* The actual calculation of bonus amounts may be the most controversial allocation decision the task force has to make since it effects the dollar amount of bonuses to each employee. You have three primary methods for calculating each individual's payout:

Equal shares.

The absolute amount in the bonus pool is divided by the number of participating employees so that each employee receives the same amount.

$$\frac{\$ \text{ Pool}}{\# \text{ Employees}} = \$ \text{ Bonus per employee}$$

Hours worked.

In this case, the absolute amount in the bonus pool is divided by the total hours worked by participating employees to arrive at an amount of bonus due per hour worked. Each employee's payment is equal to the amount per hour times the hours that employee worked.

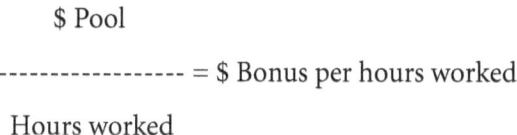

$Pool

-------------------- = $ Bonus per hours worked

Hours worked

Percent of total income.

The amount in the bonus pool is divided by total wages (regular plus overtime) of the participating employees to arrive at a bonus percentage. Thus, a bonus pool amount of 10 percent of total wages results in each employee receiving a 10 percent bonus—their individual wages for the period multiplied by 0.10.

$ Bonus Pool

---------------------------- = % W2 earnings per employee

$ Participating payroll
(W2 earnings)

In most cases, employees prefer payments based on equal shares or hours worked, however the most frequently used method is percent of income. The reason for this choice is that the latter is the only sure way for a company to remain in compliance with the Fair Labor Standards Act.

The Fair Labor Standards Act (FLSA) says that bonuses and commissions paid to employees must be included as part of regular pay when calculating the rate for overtime (one and one-half times the regular rate for hours over forty in one week). Only seven types of payments are excluded from this requirement:

1. Gifts;

2. Christmas bonuses;

3. Special occasion bonuses;

4. Payments to profit sharing;

5. Thrift plans;

6. Savings plans; and

7. Irrevocable contributions to a bona fide trust.

Gainsharing payments are not among these exclusions. The only sure way to avoid problems under the Fair Labor Standards Act is to make bonus payments a percentage of total wages (regular plus overtime).

CAUTIONARY NOTE. If you choose a method of payout other than percent of total income, you should have the payout method reviewed carefully by your attorney to ensure you are not in violation of the FLSA or obtain permission in advance from the Department of Labor.

Plant X Gainsharing Plan Documentation

Section 1.6—Allocation Basis

Bonus payments will be made in a separate check at the end of the month following the gainsharing accounting period. The bonus amount will be calculated as a percentage of each eligible person's gross wages for that period, including overtime and shift premium but excluding any relocation reimbursement or education assistance. The bonus percentage will be a ratio of the total bonus amount earned for the period divided by the total labor costs of plan participants for that period.

Section 1.7—Performance Period

The performance period refers to the time period over which gains are calculate, the amount of time allowed for calculating payments due, and the administrative time required to issue checks. Most gainsharing plans calculate gains and make payments monthly. Some companies base gains on quarterly or even semiannual performance, however longer periods tend to be less motivating than shorter ones.

A few plans calculate gains based upon a four-week rolling average of performance or by some other more complicated method. Generally, these plans are more difficult for employees to understand and for the company to administer.

In establishing the performance period for your program, keep the following pros and cons of frequent payments in mind.

1. Frequent payment has greater motivational impact since the payment is closer to the time of performance of the behavior that led to the gain.

2. Frequent payments may mean that people receive smaller individual checks.

3. If performance is seasonal, frequent payments may not be possible without a significant holdback to protect against spikes in performance.

4. Frequent payments may mean higher administrative costs.

When the average bonus check will be small, you may want to delay payment and include it with the bonus from some future period. (See our example on the next page.) In addition, you should remember that gainsharing bonuses are intended as reinforcers and must follow all of the rules of positive reinforcement to be effective. This includes the rule that reinforcers should be provided as close to the time of performance of the behavior as possible. (If you are unfamiliar with the rules of reinforcement, we suggest you consult Boyett & Conn, *Maximum Performance Management*, pages 137-175, Boyett & Boyett, *Guru Guide*, pages 263-274, and Aubrey Daniels, *Bringing Out the Best in People*, (McGraw-Hill, 1994).)

Plant X Gainsharing Plan Documentation

Section 1.7—Performance Period

From the standpoint of motivation, the performance period for the group incentive/gainsharing program should be as short as possible. From the standpoint of measurement, the period should be long enough to minimize distortions caused by abnormal events, errors, measurement limitations or operational variability. Since variability is not a particular problem at *Plant X*, the Gainsharing Task Force determined that the performance period should be monthly.

When *Plant X* earns a bonus, employees will receive their bonus check on or before the last working day of the month following the end of the month during which the bonus was earned, provided the average bonus check is $25.00 or more. If the average bonus check is less than $25.00, bonuses will be held until the next month during which a bonus is earned and added to the bonus amount earned during that month.

Section 1.8—Holdback Provision

Many gainsharing companies include a provision to hold back a portion of employee bonuses to protect against short-term peaks in performance and to encourage employee concern about productivity gains over the long term. The danger from the company's viewpoint is that unusual conditions might result in very large bonuses for a few months of the year while productivity over the entire year does not improve or even worsens.

The gainsharing task force should consider the advisability of a holdback provision in the gainsharing plan, including the percentage of the bonus pool that should be held in reserve to protect the company from paying out substantial bonuses while absorbing large looses as in scenario #3 below.

Here is an illustration of what can happen based upon three scenarios offered by John Belcher in his book *Gainsharing.*

Scenario # 1:

Quarter	1st	2nd	3rd	4th	Year
TotalGain/Loss	$100	$100	($100)	$100	$200
Employee Share @ 50%	50	50	0	50	150
Company Share @ 50%	50	50	(100)	50	50

[Note: In the case of a loss, employees receive no bonus and the company absorbs the loss.]

Scenario # 2:

Quarter	1st	2nd	3rd	4th	Year
Total Gain/Loss	$100	$100	($200)	$100	$200
Employee Share @ 50%	50	50	0	50	150
Company Share @ 50%	50	50	(200)	50	(50)

Scenario # 3:

Quarter	1st	2nd	3rd	4th	Year
Total Gain/Loss	$100	$100	($400)	$100	$200
Employee Share @ 50%	50	50	0	50	150
Company Share @ 50%	50	50	(400)	50	(150)

When there is a holdback provision, the percentage placed in reserve by gain-sharing plans typically ranges from a low of 10 percent to as much as 70 percent. Experience indicates that 20 percent works well, since that level does not appear excessive to employees but at the same time places enough of the bonus at risk to encourage employees to adopt a long-term view. Higher holdback percentages might be appropriate if the company experiences seasonal fluctuations or has a history of erratic performance, or if spikes in performance are a concern to corporate management.

If the task force adopts a holdback provision, there are a number of other related issues they will need to resolve, including the ones below.

1. *What will happen to the funds held back?* Usually holdback funds are placed in a special account and paid out at year's end provided performance for the total year is positive. These payments are usually made in the form of a separate check.

2. *If a loss occurs during a period when performance falls below the base for gainsharing (loss against target), should the holdback be charged for the loss?* Many plans charge 100 percent of any loss against the holdback account.

3. *If there are insufficient funds in the holdback to cover the loss, should the holdback be allowed to go negative?* Many plans do allow the account to go negative.

4. *Should the holdback be the same for positive and negative periods, or should it increase for negative periods so that the funds in holdback absorb some or all of the loss?* Many plans hold back only 20 percent in positive periods but charge the full amount of any loss against the holdback account during a negative period.

5. *If the holdback is negative at the end of the year, should the company absorb the loss and "zero out" the account for the start of the new year, or should the*

loss carry over? Normally, the account is zeroed out so each gainsharing year the holdback account starts at zero.

6.   *Finally, who is eligible to receive holdback payments at year's end? Are just those on the payroll at that time eligible, and if so, what about retirees, laid-off workers, or employees on extended leave?* In general, only those employees on the payroll at the end of the fiscal year are eligible to receive holdback payments. Some exceptions might include employees who retire and the estates of employees who die during the year.

Plant X Gainsharing Plan Documentation

Section 1.8—Holdback Provision

Holdback is a predetermined percentage of the total bonus pool that is held back (not distributed) each gainsharing accounting period to protect against any periods in which a loss against the goal occurs. The holdback pool will be kept in a separate account. Any money remaining in the pool at the end of the fiscal accounting year will be paid to the participants in the form of a separate check. The allocation of this pool to each participant will be based on the total gross earnings for the entire fiscal accounting year and will be calculated in the same manner in which the monthly bonuses are calculated. Payment will be made by the end of the first calendar month of the new fiscal year.

If a loss is incurred against the target during a month, then the amount of that loss will be deducted from the holdback account to the extent that there are funds in the account to cover the loss. In the event that there are insufficient funds in the account to cover the loss, the full amount of the loss will still be applied against the account, and the account balance will be allowed to fall to a negative amount equal to the unabsorbed portion of the loss. If at the end of a fiscal accounting year the account balance is negative, then the company will absorb the loss so that the account begins the next fiscal year with a zero balance. In either case, the account will begin a fiscal year with a zero balance, with no previous gains/losses being carried over to the next year. In no case will a bonus already paid to participants be recalled to cover losses in a subsequent fiscal accounting period. Any funds remaining in the account at the end of the fiscal accounting year will be paid out to the participants on a prorated basis and based on total gross earning for the fiscal accounting year.

Due to the uncertainty of the variability of potential gains, the holdback will be 20 percent of the bonus pool. This holdback percentage will still put a substantial portion of the gains immediately into the hands of the participants in the form of bonuses, while at the same time putting aside funds to protect against those fiscal accounting periods in which a loss occurs. The holdback percentage will be reviewed annually and revisions will be made as actual experience dictates.

Only employees on the payroll at the end of the fiscal year, with the exception of retirees, laid-off employees, employees on military leave, the estate of employees who die, and employees on leave of absence, will be eligible for holdback payout. Employees whose employment is terminated for any reason will have no claim to their contribution to the holdback account.

In summary, the following points illustrate payout provisions for the holdback account:

If an employee is terminated or quits before year-end, that person will be ineligible for the holdback payout. His or her share will be paid to the remaining eligible employees based on gross earnings for the fiscal gainsharing year.

Employees who retire during the year will be eligible to receive a share of the holdback account based upon the calculated percent multiplied by their gross earnings for the year.

The estate of employees who die during the year will receive a share of the holdback account based upon the calculated percentage multiplied by the employee's gross earnings for the year.

Pay that employees receive during the 90-day probationary period will not be included in their gross pay for the year for holdback account payout calculation.

The holdback check will be paid out to participants along with the check for the final month of the old fiscal year.

Section 1.9—Sunset Provision

Most gainsharing plans provide for a formal review of the program after the first year and state that the program will lapse unless a specific decision is made by management to continue. By establishing the need for a formal review, the company ensures that it will have an opportunity to decide whether to continue, modify or terminate the gainsharing program in the future.

Plant X Gainsharing Plan Documentation

Section 1.9—Sunset Provision

The incentive/gainsharing plan is intended to serve as a pilot program for *Plant X*. Therefore, the company reserves the right to review the effectiveness of the plan at the end of the first year of operation and annually thereafter. At such times, the company may terminate, modify, or continue the plan without changes, as it deems appropriate.

Before implementation, the bonus plan will be fully explained and then a survey will be taken of *Plant X* employees. Employee concerns will then be addressed during implementation. At the end of the first year, the work force will again be surveyed. The company will have the option at that time and thereafter to continue, modify or terminate the plan. This plan may be replaced by a new or modified plan that is deemed better suited to prevailing conditions or which responds to employee concerns.

Section 1.10—Adjustment Provisions

The gainsharing plan should contain provisions for changes that may occur in the way business is conducted. Such provisions might include what would happen if the company's products or services change, if major capital investments are made, or if new technology is introduced. You should consider provisions for any potential changes that might affect the plan. For example, if gains are made as a result of the introduction of new technology, should employees share in part of these gains? Try to anticipate what might happen to make the plan obsolete or that might result in windfall gains. Decide how to deal with each of these events. For example, you might adjust the gainsharing baseline by the amount the new technology is expected to effect performance. Alternatively, if you have a financial formula you might include depreciation as a cost in the formula and absorb at least part of the impact of the investment that way.

Plant X Gainsharing Plan Documentation

Section 1.10—Adjust Provision

It is necessary that the gainsharing program be equipped to deal with all future management-initiated operational changes. When and if changes are implemented by management that affect the gainsharing target, management reserves the right to adjust the gainsharing target as necessary to compensate for such changes. Examples of changes that might result in a change in the gainsharing target under this provision include, but are not limited to the following:

- Installation of more modern equipment that would result in an increase in throughput;

- A change in product packaging that significantly reduces packaging time; or

- Any major capital investment by the company that results in the creation of windfall bonuses for employees.

The necessity and rationale for any such changes, which are expected to be infrequent, will be explained to employees in team or company-wide meetings before they are implemented.

Section 1.11—Buyback Provision

The task force should consider what options the company should have in changing the basis of gainsharing calculations for reasons other than the management-initiated changes discussed in the previous section. For example, the company may want to reserve the right to adjust the basis or target if one or more of the following occurs:

- Unit costs increase rather than decrease,

- The company experiences increased competitive pressure from a lower cost producer, or

- Significant price deterioration occurs in the marketplace.

Under such circumstances, the company may choose to buy back or change the basis by making a one-time payment to employees that is equal to some percentage of difference between the old and new baselines.

Plant X Gainsharing Plan Documentation

Section 1.11—Buyback Provision

If *Plant X* decides that the gainsharing target needs to be changed because of increased competitive pressure, significant price deterioration in the marketplace or for other reasons that are outside employee and management control, then the company shall have the right to change the target by *buying back* 50 percent of the difference between the old and new targets. For example, if the difference between the old target and the new target is $.05 per unit, the company will make a one-time, lump sum payment to employees equal to $.025 times last year's total units. The new target will remain in effect for future gainsharing calculations unless bought back under the same provisions or changed as a result of management-initiated operational changes (see Adjustment Provision).

Section 1.12—Bonus Ceiling

In this step, the task force must decide whether there will be a cap on amounts of the bonuses that can be earned during any single period. For example, the maximum bonus might be 10 percent, 20 percent, or 30 percent, with any gains in excess of the cap being lost or credited to the reserve (holdback) fund. If you establish a deferred account, any amount earned in excess of the bonus ceiling is placed in that account, and funds are withdrawn from that account in any subsequent period in which there is no gain or in which the gain does not reach the bonus ceiling. For example,

	Period 1	Period 2	Period 3
Earned	25%	50%	20%
Paid	25%	30%	30%
Deferred	0%	20%	10%

Generally, a ceiling is unnecessary, provided the gainsharing formula is constructed so that gains are not too easy to make. If you choose to establish a bonus ceiling, however, you should take into consideration that large bonuses do not translate into high operating costs if the bonuses result from true productivity improvements.

Plant X Gainsharing Plan Documentation

Section 1.12—Bonus Ceiling

Group incentive/gainsharing programs provide a means for a company to move from a control- to a reward-based relationship with employees. Bonus ceilings are counterproductive to this effort and therefore inappropriate as long as relevant data used for setting targets and calculating gains are accurate, historically meaningful, and based on good standards. As long as a real gain— not a windfall—is realized, the amount of wages paid should be irrelevant.

High, overall, total compensation for employees, including variable pay from incentive or gainsharing programs, does not necessarily result in high operating costs. The real test is the productivity of the employees earning that high, total compensation. Consequently, *Plant* X will have no ceiling on the amount of gainsharing bonus employees may earn.

Section 1.13—Sharing Ratio

The sharing ratio, as defined by the gainsharing plan, specifies how the company and the employees will share in the savings achieved through gainsharing. This ratio must be fair to the company and to employees. The most equitable split, both to the company and employees, is a 50/50 split. However, other ratios (60/40, 75/25, and so on) are acceptable ratios, provided you justify your decision.

In order to be equitable, the sharing ratio should meet three major criteria.

1. The ratio must put a sufficient share of the gains into the employee bonus pool to remain attractive and create a sufficiently strong incentive for improvement among the participant group.

2. The ratio must return a sufficient share of the gains to the company to maintain an acceptable level of profitability from improvements.

3. The ratio must be logical and justifiable to plan participants, corporate management and other relevant stakeholders.

In his book *Gainsharing*, John Belcher suggests other factors to consider in setting the sharing ratio:

• If the formula is tightly designed so that you are reasonably confident that it captures only improvements that employees themselves cause then a high sharing ratio to employees would be appropriate. If on the other hand, the formula is more general and there may be factors affecting the formula that are out of employee control then you many want to keep the employees' share low.

• If the site is very capital intensive, then you may want to keep the employee share low in order to retain more of the gains for future capital investment.

• The baseline itself may make a difference. Belcher suggests the following rules:

If the base line is...	Then the employee share should be...
Tough	High
Easy	Low
Rolling/ratchet up	High
Fixed	Low
Historical baseline	Low
Target baseline	High

Finally, Belcher suggests that if you are concerned about having large payouts to employees when the company is not performing well financially then you could make the sharing ratio dependent upon some other measure. For example:

ROI	Employee Share
High	50%
Average	35
Low	20
Negative	0

Or

Gross profit to plan	Employee Share
+2% or more over plan	50%
On plan to 2% over plan	40
-2% under plan to on plan	30
Greater than 2% under plan	0

Plant X Gainsharing Plan Documentation

Section 1.13—Sharing Ratio

After much discussion, management has decided that the sharing ratio for *Plant X* will be set at 50/50, with half of any gains going to the company and half going into the bonus pool. No logical justification for another ratio (60/40, 40/60, 75/25, etc.) has been presented to date, so the 50/50 ratio is considered the fairest point at which to start a pilot gainsharing program. However, the company retains the right to change this ratio as part of the sunset provision of this program.

Section 1.14—Administrative Details

In this step, the task force will make a number of decisions concerning how the program will be administered during the first year. For example:

1. If the program starts in mid-accounting year, will the first year under gainsharing be shortened so that the holdback is paid out at the end of the current accounting year, thus bringing the gainsharing year into sync with the accounting year?

2. What about any training or start-up costs associated with gainsharing? Must employees absorb them? Must training costs be overcome before gains are paid or will the company absorb these costs?

3. Is there a need for a transition plan from any individual incentive(s) to gainsharing? How will high performers under the old individual incentive plan be protected from possible losses in their total income? You may choose to implement a skill-based pay system to protect high performers. (See Boyett & Conn, *Maximum Performance Management*, pages 240-242 for an explanation.)

Plant X Gainsharing Plan Documentation

Section 1.14—Administrative Details

What kind of first year adjustments will there be to the gainsharing program?

> Current planning calls for gainsharing to begin in the 9th accounting period of the current fiscal year (February 28, fiscal month of March). In order to bring the gainsharing year into sync with the fiscal year, the first gainsharing year will be only four months long and will end at the end of the current fiscal year. After that, the gainsharing year and fiscal year will be the same.

Who will absorb training costs associated with gainsharing?

> When gainsharing begins, training costs for team training and any cross training of operators will be reflected in the operating costs of the plant and will be reflected in the gainsharing calculation.

How will employees be transitioned from any individual incentive to gainsharing?

> The gainsharing task force has decided that as the plan moves from an individual incentive to a group incentive some provision should be made to protect high performers from experiencing a loss of income and to encourage job flexibility. Therefore, effective with the introduction of gainsharing, operators on individual incentive will be frozen at their current year-to-date efficiencies and paid a straight hourly rate through a cross training period. Operators will be given the opportunity to learn a set of inspect/repair machine maintenance skills. Under a simplified skill-based pay system, qualifying multi-skilled operators will be paid a pay-for-knowledge supplement to their base pay. See our pay-for-knowledge documentation for details.

3

Gainsharing Calculation

A critical responsibility of the task force is the development of the formula to be used for calculating gains. The feasibility study will provide some suggestions about the key areas of performance that should be covered in the formula, as will the statement of objectives. Both should be reviewed at this point. The task force should also review the sample formulas in this chapter.

Formulas are generally of two types—performance based and financial based. As you might expect, there are considerable arguments for and against each type, however in our opinion, there is no right or wrong formula or type of formula.

Criteria for a Good Formula

In developing the gainsharing formula, the task force should consider the objectives for the gainsharing plan they developed earlier, as well as the following criteria for a good formula:

Fair to the company.

The first test of a gainsharing formula has to be whether it is a true measure of performance over time and whether success on that measure will enable the company better to achieve its strategic objectives. Financial incentives are very powerful tools, therefore you have to ensure that when gains are earned, the company benefits as well as employees. You do not want a formula with which employees are making bonuses at the expense of the company. In the long term, the company can be severely damaged, and no one will win.

Fair to the employees.

Another test is whether or not the formula is fair to employees. Employees need the opportunity to make gains, provided they work harder or smarter. They have to be able to make a difference through changes in their behavior. If the formula includes too many extraneous variables outside of employee control, the whole gainsharing effort can fail. Employees may simply quit trying.

Understandable to employees.

Employees must be able to understand how the formula works and how their behavior affects performance as measured by the formula. An elaborate and sophisticated formula that no one but the comptroller can understand will fail because employees do not understand how gains are derived. Ideally, the gainsharing formula should be tied as closely to possible to what people physically do. Employees should be able to predict whether or not they will obtain a gain for any given performance period simply by observing what is happening around them day to day. For example, if the formula is tied to some measurement of products shipped, employees will see the shipments occurring daily. They will have a sense of the gains or losses that will affect the calculations for that period.

Easy to administer.

A good gainsharing formula should be easy to calculate based upon information that is already available to you on a regular and timely basis. You do not want to create elaborate new accounting systems to support the gainsharing program. Additionally, you need to pay bonuses as soon after the end of the performance period as possible. Gainsharing bonuses are reinforcers, and they are subject to all the rules governing the effectiveness of reinforcers. You will recall that one of these rules is that the reinforcer must be given as close to the performance incident as possible.

Flexible.

A good gainsharing formula should be flexible. The environment in which most companies compete changes rapidly today. As a result, company goals, objectives, and priorities change. If the gainsharing formula is to last, it has to accommodate these changes and not lock the company into rewarding behavior and performance that was appropriate once, but is no longer consistent with company goals and strategies.

Useful in isolating problem areas.

Finally, a good gainsharing formula should help employee problem-solving teams isolate potential problem areas and should provide useful information concerning the possible causes of low productivity. Ideally, the calculation itself will suggest particular product lines, materials cost, and so on that are causing or contributing to poor performance. As a result, the formula will help direct problem-solving efforts.

Establish the Gainsharing Target

Part of the development of a formula is the establishment of a baseline from which gains will be calculated. Bonuses are paid if performance is better than this baseline. Here there are two possible methods of calculation:

Historical baseline.

Average performance is calculated over a period ranging from six months to as much as five years. Obviously, the length of time examined depends upon a number of factors, including the availability of data, the length of time needed to smooth out seasonal or cyclical fluctuations, and so on.

If you have limited or poor historical data, you should consider using a moving average for your gainsharing target. For example, the target might be set at the average of the last six months. Each month you drop the oldest month and add a new month to compute the target.

If it is possible for volume levels to effect performance, you should do a regression analysis (or, at a minimum, a scatter plot) to determine how volume might influence payouts. If you determine that the gainsharing formula is sensitive to volume, you have three options:

(1) Put a cap or bonus ceiling on the payout (See our discussion of Bonus Ceiling);

(2) Expand the performance period to smooth out the fluctuations in volume (See out discussion of Performance Period); or

(3)   Reduce the share of the gain going to employees (See our discussion of Sharing Ratio).

Employees usually view historical targets as fair and equitable since they are based upon actual prior performance. Perhaps that is why they are used in approximately 60% of gainsharing plans.

Target baseline

This approach is frequently used when past performance is considered to be poor. The argument is that gains should not be paid until a certain target level is reached, regardless of past performance. Target baselines are most appropriate if (1) the site is uncompetitive or in financial difficulties, or (2) the site is new so no historical data exists.

Once a baseline is selected, the task force must determine whether that baseline will remain fixed—all future gains will be measured from the same base performance level—or will change over time. If the base will be allowed to change, the task force should also decide whether it will be stepped up by some predetermined level each year or change according to some recalculation of average performance—for example, be based upon a rolling average of the last X number of periods, such as we suggested when historical data is poor.

Regardless of whether the base is fixed or will step up, the task force should consider management's option to change the base under certain circumstances such as an increase in unit costs, an increase in competitive pressure from a lower cost producer, or a significant price deterioration in the marketplace. In such situations, the company should opt to buy back a change in the base by making a one-time payment to employees equal to some percentage of the difference between the old and the new baseline. (See our discussion of buyback.)

Sample Formulas

With these rules and concepts in mind, let us look at some examples, starting with a simple financial based formula.

Sample Formula: Single Ratio—Labor Cost to Sales Value of Production

Suppose *Company A*'s major cost is for labor (payroll cost plus fringe benefits), and a good measurement of its output is the sales value of production. Also, let's assume that neither the input measure (labor costs) nor the output measure (sales value of production) are significantly affected by extraneous factors, so that the ratio of labor cost to sales value of production is a good measure of performance over time. Given this situation, *Company A* could use a standard Scanlon formula called the "Single Ratio" to calculate any gains.

If it used a Single Ratio formula, the company would first determine what the ratio of labor costs was to sales value of production during a base period, and then use that ratio to determine an allowed labor cost during the current period. Any savings in actual labor costs, when compared to the allowed labor cost for a given month, would be a productivity gain and could be shared with employees. A sample calculation might be as follows:

First, *Company A* calculates what is called an historical base ratio. This is simply the existing ratio of labor costs to sales value of production before installing gainsharing. Let's say that *Company A*'s historical base ratio is the following:

Labor Costs	$2,952,000	
--------------	--------------	= 20% Base Ratio
Sales Value of Production	$14,760,000	

Having established a base ratio, *Company A* then determines each month whether or not there is any gain. The monthly calculation might be something like Exhibit 3-1.

Exhibit 3-1: Sample Single Ratio—Labor Cost to Sales Value of Production

BASE PERIOD CALCULATION		
Labor Costs	$246,000.00	Actual Base Period
Sales Value of Production	$1,230,000.00	Actual Base Period
Base Ratio	20.00%	Labor Costs / Sales Value of Production
Company % Share of Bonus Pool	25.00%	Established by Gainsharing Task Force
Employee % Share of Bonus Pool	75.00%	Established by Gainsharing Task Force
Holdback Percentage	25.00%	Established by Gainsharing Task Force
CALCULATION FOR MONTH		
Sales for Month	$1,560,000.00	Actual for Month
Minus Returns, Allowances, Discounts, etc.	$35,700.00	Actual for Month
Net Sales	$1,524,300.00	Sales minus Returns, etc.
Plus Increase in Inventory at Selling Price	$178,500.00	Actual for Month
Value of Production	$1,702,800.00	Net Sales plus Increase in Inventory
Allowed Payroll Costs	$340,560.00	Base Ratio x Value of Production
Actual Payroll Costs	$293,521.00	Actual for Month
Bonus Pool	$47,039.00	Allowed Payroll minus Actual Payroll
Company Share of Bonus Pool	$11,759.75	Bonus Pool x Company Percent
Employee Share of Bonus Pool	$35,279.25	Bonus Pool x Employee Percent
Holdback for Deficit Months	$8,819.81	Employee Share x Holdback Percent
Employee Share for Immediate Distribution	$26,459.44	Employee Share minus Holdback
Total Participating Payroll (W2 Earnings)	$253,125.00	Actual for Month
BONUS PERCENTAGE	10.45%	Employee Share for Distribution / Participating Payroll

Notice several things about the above calculation. First, the gain and resulting bonus made by employees resulted from a true increase in productivity from the base period. Although labor costs went up by over $47,000—from $246,000 during the base period to $293,521 during the current period—the sales value of production increased by $520,321—from $1,230,000 to $1,702,800. Given the historical base ratio, *Company A* would have expected payroll costs to be 20 percent of the sales value of production, or $340,560 ($1,702,800 X 0.20). However, labor costs were actually only $293,521, which represents a savings or productivity gain of $47,039 for that month. Employees thus produced much more for very little additional increase in cost. As a result, a bonus was earned.

A second thing to notice from our example is how the amount of any gain was calculated and how much of the gain was returned to employees. The amount of the bonus earned in our example was equal to 75 percent of the difference between the expected or allowed labor costs for that level of production and the actual labor costs. As we said earlier, many gainsharing plans divide any gains equally between employees and the company, however other plans allocate as little as 25 percent or as much as 75 percent of the gains to employees.

Third, note that the company did not immediately distribute the employees' entire share of the gain. In this case, the company held 25 percent back. As explained earlier, the purpose of the holdback provision is to protect the company from short-term spikes in productivity, during which large bonuses might be made only to be followed by deficit months. (See our discussion of the holdback provision.)

Finally, note that in our example the amount remaining in the bonus pool after holdback is expressed as a percentage of the total employee payroll. In this case, the amount of bonus each employee receives will be equal to 10.45 percent of his or her total wages (regular plus overtime). Thus, employees with higher total wages receive a larger portion of the funds in the bonus pool. This practice is another common feature of gainsharing plans. Though many employees object to this particular feature, arguing that bonuses should be distributed equally, most companies end up with this distribution method since it is the easiest way to ensure that the plan is in compliance with the Fair Labor Standards Act. (See our discussion of Allocation Basis.)

Sample Formula: Split Ratio—Labor Cost to Sales Value of Production

As we said, a single ratio formula can work well if the ratio of labor cost to sales value of production is a good measure of performance over time. However, a single ratio formula can become outdated quickly if the product mix changes. In such cases, the company might want to use a second type of Scanlon formula called the Split Ratio formula as shown in Exhibit 3-2.

Exhibit 3-2: Split Ratio Calculation

BASE RATIOS

Product A	30.00%	Calculated from Base Period
Product B	10.00%	Calculated from Base Period
Company % Share of Bonus Pool	25.00%	Established by Task Force
Employee % Share of Bonus Pool	75.00%	Established by Task Force
Holdback Percentage	25.00%	Established by Task Force

CALCULATION FOR MONTH

SALES FOR MONTH

Product A	$800,000.00	Actual for Period
Product B	$850,000.00	Actual for Period
TOTAL SALES	$1,650,000.00	Product A plus Product B

MINUS RETURNS, ALLOWANCES,
DISCOUNTS, ETC.

Product A	$18,570.00	Actual for Period
Product B	$18,830.00	Actual for Period
TOTAL RETURNS, ETC.	$37,400.00	Product A plus Product B
NET SALES		Total Sales minus Returns, et
Product A	$781,430.00	
Product B	$831,170.00	
TOTAL NET SALES	$1,612,600.00	

PLUS INCREASE IN INVENTORY
AT SELLING PRICE

Product A	$92,950.00	Actual for Period
Product B	$93,750.00	Actual for Period
TOTAL INCREASE IN INVENTORY	$186,700.00	Product A plus Product B
VALUE OF PRODUCTION	Net Sales plus Increase in Inventory	

VALUE OF PRODUCTION

Product A	$874,380.00	
Product B	$924,920.00	
TOTAL	$1,799,300.00	Value of Production x Base R

SPLIT RATIO CALCULATION (CONTINUED)

ALLOWED PAYROLL COSTS		
Product A	$262,314.00	
Product B	$92,492.00	
TOTAL ALLOWED PAYROLL	$354,806.00	
ACTUAL PAYROLL COSTS	$312,950.00	Actual for Period
BONUS POOL	$41,856.00	Allowed Payroll minus Actual Payroll
COMPANY SHARE OF BONUS POOL	$10,464.00	Bonus Pool x Company %
EMPLOYEE SHARE OF BONUS POOL	$31,392.00	Bonus Pool x Employee %
HOLDBACK FOR DEFICIT MONTHS	$7,848.00	Employee Share x Holdback %
EMPLOYEE SHARE FOR IMMEDIATE DISTRIBUTION	$23,544.00	Employee Share minus Holdback
TOTAL PARTICIPATING PAYROLL	$253,125.00	Actual for Period
BONUS PERCENTAGE	9.30%	Employee Share for Distribution

Notice that the Split Ratio formula works very much like the Single Ratio formula except that it breaks out the Sales Value of Production and Payroll Costs by product line. Therefore, it can react to changes in product mix. The biggest problem with the Split Ratio formula is that many companies have trouble allocating cost across product lines.

Sample Formula: Multicost Ratio

A third Scanlon-type formula is called the Multicost Ratio. It is a much broader measure of performance that takes into consideration costs other than labor costs. See Exhibit 3-3 for an example of the Muticost Ratio formula.

Exhibit 3-3: Multicost Ratio Calculation

BASE PERIOD CALCULATION

    TOTAL COSTS

Labor	$2,952,000.00	Actual Base Period
Materials and Supplies	$7,620,000.00	Actual Base Period
Other Costs	$1,236,000.00	Actual Base Period
BASE PERIOD TOTAL COSTS	$11,808,000.00	
Base Period Sales Value of Production	$14,760,000.00	Actual Base Period
Base Ratio	80.00%	Total Costs / Sales Value of Production
Company % Share of Bonus Pool	25.00%	Established by Task Force
Employee % Share of Bonus Pool	75.00%	Established by Task Force
Holdback Percentage	25.00%	Established by Task Force

CALCULATION FOR MONTH

Sales for Month	$1,650,000.00	Actual for Month
Minus Returns, Allowances, Discounts, etc.	$37,500.00	Actual for Month
Net Sales	$1,612,500.00	Sales minus Returns, etc.
Plus Increase in Inventory at Selling Price	$187,500.00	Actual for Month
Value of Production	$1,800,000.00	Net Sales plus Increase in Inventory
ALLOWED EXPENSES	$1,440,000.00	Base Ratio x Value of Production
ACTUAL EXPENSES		
Labor	$315,000.00	Actual for Month
Materials and Supplies	$756,000.00	Actual for Month
Other Costs	$324,000.00	Actual for Month
TOTAL ACTUAL EXPENSES	$1,395,000.00	
BONUS POOL	$45,000.00	Allowed Expenses minus Actual Expenses
Company Share of Bonus Pool	$11,250.00	Bonus Pool x Company Percent
Employee Share of Bonus Pool	$33,750.00	Bonus Pool x Employee Percent
Holdback for Deficit Months	$8,437.50	Employee Share x Holdback Percent
Employee Share for Immediate Distribution	$25,312.50	Employee Share minus Holdback
Total Participating Payroll (W2 Earnings)	$253,125.00	
BONUS PERCENTAGE	10.00%	Employee Share for Distribution / Participating Payroll

Sample Formula: Value Added or Rucker® Plan

Developed by economist Alan Rucker in the 1930s, the Rucker ® Plan calculation is based upon the finding that the ratio of labor costs to the sales value of production is relatively stable across time in most manufacturing environments. Whereas the Scanlon formulas relate net sales to labor costs, the Rucker® calculation relates labor costs to value-added (sales value of production minus outside purchases). See Exhibit 3-4 for an example of a Rucker® Plan calculation.

Exhibit 3-4: Value-Added or Rucker® Plan Calculation

BASE PERIOD CALCULATIONS

Sales Value of Production	$23,400,000.00	**Actual Base Period**
Minus Outside Purchases	$14,040,000.00	
BASE PERIOD VALUE ADDED	$9,360,000.00	
BASE PERIOD LABOR COSTS	$3,744,000.00	
Base Ratio	40.00%	**Base Period Labor Costs / Base Period Value Added**
Company % Share of Bonus Pool	50.00%	**Established by Task Force**
Employee % Share of Bonus Pool	50.00%	**Established by Task Force**
Holdback Percentage	20.00%	**Established by Task Force**

CALCULATION FOR MONTH

Sales Value of Production	$2,100,000.00	**Actual for Month**
Minus Outside Purchases	$1,155,000.00	**Actual for Month**
Value Added	$945,000.00	**Sales minus Outside Purchases**
Allowed Labor Costs	$378,000.00	**Value Added x Base Ratio**
Actual Labor Costs	$314,732.25	**Actual for Month**
BONUS POOL	$63,267.75	**Base Ratio x Value of Production**
Company Share of Bonus Pool	$31,633.88	**Bonus Pool x Company Percent**
Employee Share of Bonus Pool	$31,633.88	**Bonus Pool x Employee Percent**
Holdback for Deficit Months	$6,326.78	**Employee Share x Holdback Percent**
Employee Share for Immediate Distribution	$25,307.10	**Employee Share minus Holdback**
Total Participating Payroll	$253,125.00	**Actual for Month**
BONUS PERCENTAGE	9.99%	**Employee Share / Participating Payroll**

Sample Formula: Improshare®

The Improshare® formula was developed by Mitch Fein, a consultant and industrial engineer in the early 1970s. Improshare® is a physical rather than financial formula. Instead of relating labor costs to production, Improshare® compares labor hours expended in the current period to standard or expected labor hours given the current units of production.

Exhibit 3-5: Improshare® Calculation

BASE PERIOD CALCULATION

   A. STANDARD HOURS PER UNIT

(Production Hours / Production Units)

	Production Hours	Production Units	Standard Hours Per Unit
Product A	400.00	400.00	1.00
Product B	1,000.00	500.00	2.00
Product C	800.00	200.00	4.00

   B. STANDARD VALUE HOURS

       (Units x Standard Hours per Unit)

	Production Units	Standard Hours per Unit	Standard Value Hours (SVH)
Product A	400.00	1.00	400.00
Product B	500.00	2.00	1,000.00
Product C	200.00	4.00	800.00
TOTAL STANDARD VALUE HOURS (SVH)			2,200.00
EMPLOYEE BONUS PERCENTAGE			50.00%

C. BASE PRODUCTIVITY FACTOR

Total Production Hours	2,200.00 **Actual for Base period**
Total Non-Production Hours	1,000.00 **Actual for Base period**
Total Actual Hours	3,200.00
Total Standard Hours Earned	2,200.00
Base Productivity Factor (BPF)	1.45 **Total Actual Hours / Total Standard Hours**

Improshare® Calculation (Continued)			
MONTHLY BONUS CALCULATION			
PRODUCT	A	B	C
Units	500.00	550.00	250.00
STV Hours	1.00	2.00	4.00
BPF	1.45	1.45	1.45
STANDARD HOURS EARNED	725.00	1,595.00	1,450.00
TOTAL IMPROSHARE HOURS EARNED	3,770.00	Sum of Standard Hours Earned Products A, B, and C	
ACTUAL HOURS WORKED	3,000.00	Actual for Period	
HOURS GAINED	770.00	Total Improshare Hours Earned—Actual Hours	
EMPLOYEE BONUS HOURS	385.00	Hours Gained x Employee Bonus Percent	
BONUS PERCENTAGE	12.83%	Employee Bonus Hours / Actual Hours Worked	

Sample Formula: Customized—Controllable Cost Per Unit of Production

The Scanlon, Rucker®, and Improshare® formulas are standard or generic formulas. Many companies have used such formulas with little, in any, modification. However, none of these standard formulas may be right for your particular situation. In that case, you may want to develop a customized formula. In this and the remaining examples, we will discuss some examples of customized formulas actual companies have used. We start with a formula that bases gainsharing bonuses on reductions in unit costs.

This company wanted to tie gainsharing to *controllable cost per unit,* which it defined as the sum of the following:

Total direct labor

+ *Total variable overhead (excluding net charges variable)*

+ *Total fixed charges*

> *(Excluding property tax and insurance,*
>
> *depreciation, travel, entertainment, relocations, employee relations, dues, subscriptions, professional fees, training and education and net charges fixed)*

+/- *Chargeable inventory carrying cost*

      ($amt. over/under plan X % inventory carrying cost for quarter)

+   *Work in process inventory carrying*

      ($ amt. over/under plan x % inventory carrying cost for quarter)

+   *Number of defective returns from customers x $37.50.*

Controllable cost per unit is defined as *controllable cost* divided by units produced for the quarter.

This plan calculated gains by comparing actual controllable cost to a target controllable cost of $.2039 per unit. Management established this target after a systematic review of historical trends in controllable cost at this plant.

The plan paid gainsharing bonuses if target controllable cost per unit exceeded actual controllable cost per unit for the quarter. The employee bonus pool consisted of 50 percent of this gain. One-half of the bonus pool was held back until year's end (See the section on Holdback). The remainder of the funds in the employee bonus pool after holdback was distributed to employees as a percentage of gross wages (See the section on Allocation). See the Exhibit 3.6 for an illustration of a monthly calculation.

Exhibit 3.6: Sample Calculation—Controllable Cost Formula

Pounds Produced	5,708,336	Actual for Month
Pounds Late Shipment	37,675	Actual for Month
Adjusted Pounds	5,670,661	Pounds Produced—Pounds Late Shipment
Total Direct Labor Cost	$120,748.00	Actual for Month
Total Variable Overhead	$601,218.00	Overtime, shift premium, holiday pay, vacation pay, supplies, outside services, utilities
Total Fixed Charges	$277,268.00	Indirect labor, rework, leases, telephone, postage
Chargeable Inventory Carrying Costs	($3,823.00)	$ Amount over or under plan
Returns Adjustment	$69,375.00	Pounds Defect Returns x $75 per Pound

Customized—Controllable Costs Formula (Continued)		
Actual Controllable Cost	$1,064,786.00	Sum of Direct Labor, Variable Overhead, Fixed Charges, and Returns Adjustment
Actual Controllable Cost per Pound	$0.1878	Controllable Cost / Adjusted Pounds
Target Controllable Cost per Pound	$0.20	Established by Gainsharing Task Force
Per Pound Savings	$0.0122	Target Controllable Cost— Actual Controllable Cost Per Pound
Total Savings (or Loss)	$69,182.06	Per Pound Savings x Adjusted Pounds
Employee Bonus Pool	$34,591.03	One Half Total Savings
Participating Payroll	$581,301.00	Actual for Month
Bonus Percentage	5.95%	Employee Bonus Pool / Participating Payroll

Sample Formula: Customized—Labor Costs Only

Our next example of a customized formula is very simple. It compares actual labor costs to target labor costs as established by the gainsharing task force based upon historical performance and competitive requirements. The company and employees share gains equally. See Exhibit 3.7 for an example.

Exhibit 3.7: Customized—Labor Costs Only

Total Labor Costs	$125,067.00	Actual for Month
First Quality Dozens	157,152	Actual for Month
Actual Dollars per Dozen	$0.7958	Total Labor Cost / First Quality Dozens
Target Dollars per Dozen	$1.0275	Established by Gainsharing Task Force
Gain/Loss per Dozen	$0.2317	Target Dollars per Dozen—Actual Dollars per Dozen
Total Gain or Loss	$36,412.00	Gain/Loss per Dozen x First Quality Dozens
Bonus Pool	$18,206.00	One half Total Gain
Holdback	$3,641.20	20 % of Bonus Pool
Monthly Bonus Pool	$14,564.80	Bonus Pool—Holdback
Participating Payroll	$125,067.00	Actual for Month
Percent Bonus	11.65%	Monthly Bonus Pool / Participating Payroll

A Service Sector—Goalsharing Formula

The above examples illustrate gainsharing formulas in a manufacturing setting. None would be particularly appropriate for a service organization. The problem with traditional gainsharing formulas for the service sector is that output measures, particularly measures of physical output, can be difficult to identify and, even if identifiable, might be less important than measures of quality, effectiveness, or customer satisfaction. However, service sector employers continue to express considerable interest in adopting gainsharing plans for their employees, and innovative ideas are being presented for adapting gainsharing to the service sector.

One of the problems in adapting gainsharing to the service sector is the tendency to lump all service sector employees into a single group. In fact, white-collar/service jobs range from the highly repetitive, easily measurable back room operations which have a predictable work flow and are very much like a factory environment, to the less repetitive and more creative knowledge-worker service environments, in which outputs are more difficult to identify and the work performed is less tangible. In the more factory-oriented white-collar/service jobs, traditional gainsharing formulas, like those we illustrate, can work very well. Traditional formulas can also work well if the service component is a profit center rather than a cost center and employees have some measure of control over revenues and costs. For example, a traditional formula might work for professionals who generate revenues from clients' fees or through charge-backs to internal operating components for services rendered and where the primary cost is labor. Such a formula might also work for employees in branch banks, employment agencies, hospitals, hotels, and other service institutions where materials, supplies, energy, and other costs are at least partially controllable by employees. If standard costs exist or can be developed—in repair shops, maintenance groups or transaction-processing areas of banks, or insurance companies—then a formula based upon the ratio of actual to standard hours might work. Thus, the problem in adapting gainsharing to the service sector is not so much with the measurable, factory-like service sector jobs or with those who directly generate revenues from the provision of services, but with the less repetitive, less tangible, knowledge-workers, particularly those who provide internal support services as cost centers. To include this latter type of service workers in gainsharing, companies have generally followed one of two basic approaches.

First, knowledge-workers who provide internal support to operating or production components of a company can be included in gainsharing by being allowed to participate in the gains experienced by the components they support. Such an approach works well for employees in areas such as production planning/scheduling, purchasing, or engineering where the support teams have a direct impact on the performance of the groups they serve in the short term. Such workers can be included for gainsharing purposes by:

- Including them as part of the operating component workforce, with their costs added to the input side of the formula;

- Not including them in calculating the bonus pool but allocating a portion of any gains to them by including them as part of the participating payroll in the payout calculation; or

- Providing them with their own separate gainsharing program with output measures tied to the operating or production component(s) performance.

Though the above approach will work for many internal support groups, it is less appropriate for internal knowledge-worker groups such as research people, systems analysts, programmers, or public relations people whose work performance is not reflected in short-term operating/production performance. For these groups, one approach is to construct the gainsharing formula based upon an objectives matrix as proposed by the American Productivity

Center. (See Carl Thor, "Knowledge Worker Gainsharing," *APC Productivity Brief* (August, 1987).)

The objectives matrix works for internal knowledge-worker employees such as those described above because it substitutes the single measure input/output ratio used in traditional gainsharing formulas with a calculation derived from weighted scores on a variety of measures, such as the following:

- Client/user ratings of service quality/effectiveness,

- Measures of compliance with internal procedures or quality standards,

- Quality measures related to rework, errors, etc.,

- Measures of on-time delivery of services,

- Measures of service delivery cost to budget or estimate, and

- Equipment and/or staff utilization measurements.

Once measures are established—preferably as the result of a group effort involving managers, supervisors, and employees—weights are assigned to reflect the relative importance of each measurement, and agreements are reached concerning service level goals and bonus points that can be earned for attaining each level. See Exhibit 3.8 for an example of an objectives matrix.

The objectives matrix is constructed and read as follows:

1. First, key indicators of performance are identified. In our sample, these are: client satisfaction, staff utilization, service delivery cost, and on-time delivery.

2. Weights are assigned to the measures to indicate their relative importance, so the total of all weights equals 100. In our example, client satisfaction and on-time delivery are assigned weights of 30 each, with staff utilization and cost weights of 20 each.

3. Next, the base period performance level is determined for each measure by examining historical data, and entering it on the matrix at performance level 3. The matrix is then completed, starting from the base level and including seven levels of performance better than the base and three levels worse than the base. Performance level 10 is used for the best performance possible or the long-term performance objective.

4. Each month, results are calculated on the key measures and entered on the objectives matrix. Reading down and across the matrix, performance levels are identified for each measure and entered at the bottom of the matrix as the current month's score. When matrix scores are multiplied by the weight for each measure, a point value is determined for the current period.

5. With this construction, the maximum point value that can be earned for any period is 1,000 points (performance level 10 X total weights of 100). The point value at the base period level is 300 (performance level 3 X total weights of 100), thus bonus points are earned if the current period point value is over 300. For example, in our sample matrix the current period point value was 650, so 350 bonus points were earned (650 minus 300 = 350).

6. To calculate the amount of money in the bonus pool and available for distribution to employees, the bonus points earned for the period are multiplied by some dollar value. In our example, each bonus point was worth $100, therefore the bonus pool was $35,000 (350 bonus points X $100 per point).

7. As with other gainsharing formulas, a portion of the bonus pool would probably be held back to protect against deficit periods, and the remainder would probably be distributed based upon the percentage that the bonus pool was of total payroll costs.

See Exhibit 3.8 for an example of an objectives matrix

Exhibit 3.8: Sample Objective Matrix—Goal Sharing / Service Calculation

PERFORMANCE LEVEL	% CLIENT SATISFACTION	% STAFF UTILIZATION	%COST TO BUDGET	% ON-TIME DELIVERY	PERFORMANCE LEVEL
CURRENT	97	93	95	97	CURRENT
10	100	100	89	100	10
9	99	99	91	99	9
8	97	98	93	98	8
7	95	97	95	97	7
6	93	96	97	96	6
5	91	95	99	95	5
4	89	94	100	94	4
3	87	93	110	93	3 — BASE
2	85	91	115	92	2
1	83	89	118	91	1
0	81	87	120	90	0
SCORE	8	3	7	7	SCORE
WEIGHT	30	20	20	30	WEIGHT
CURRENT VALUE	240	60	140	210	CURRENT VALUE — Score x Weight

TOTAL POSSIBLE POINT VALUE	1,000	Sum of Performance Level 10 x Weights
CURRENT PERIOD POINT VALUE	650	Sum of Current Value for all Measures
BASE PERIOD POINT VALUE	300	Sum of Base Performance Level 3 x Weights
BONUS POINTS EARNED	350	Current Period Point Value minus Base Period Point Value
VALUE PER BONUS POINT	$100.00	Established by Gainsharing Task Force
BONUS POOL	$35,000.00	Bonus Points Earned x Value Per Bonus Point
TOTAL PARTICIPATING PAYROLL	$350,000.00	Actual for Period
BONUS PERCENTAGE	10.00%	Bonus Pool / Total Participating Payroll

The bonus pool is calculated as follows:

Total possible point value = 1,000

(Total of weights (A + B + C + D) X (*best* performance possible),

i.e., (30 + 20 + 20 + 30) X 10 = 1,000)

Current period point value = 650

(Total of current period point values in columns A + B + C + D,

i.e., 240 + 60 + 140 + 210 = 650)

Base period point value = 300

(Total of weights (A + B + C + D) X (*base* performance level),

i.e., (30 + 20 + 20 + 30) X 3 = 300)

Bonus points earned = 350

(Current − Base, i.e., 650 − 300 = 350)

Bonus pool = $35,000

($100 per bonus point X 350 bonus points earned)

As we said above, the advantage of the objectives matrix is that it allows you to construct a gainsharing plan based upon weighted scores on a variety of measures. Bonuses are paid only if the total of weighted scores across all measures improve from the level during the base period. Additionally, once established, the objectives matrix is relatively easy to maintain and easy for employees to understand. Finally, the company can limit its risk because it can establish the maximum bonus to be paid if exceptional performance levels are reached across all measures, since the maximum possible bonus points are known in advance.

Sample Formula: Service/Goalsharing—Bonus Percentage

An alternative to the objectives matrix is to assign bonus percentages that can be earned for different levels of performance on each measure. Performance at the base level for any measure would earn zero percent. Performance above the base level would earn a percentage of total wages as a bonus, which varies based upon the relative importance of the measure and the level of performance actually obtained (good, very good, excellent, or outstanding). For example, in our sample below the maximum bonus for outstanding performance on all four measures is 12 percent. The bonus actually earned for the current period was 6 percent (3 percent client satisfaction plus zero percent on staff utilization plus 1 percent on service delivery cost plus 2 percent on on-time delivery). See Exhibit 3.9 for an example.

Exhibit 3.9: Bonus Percentages

MEASURE	BASE	GOOD	VERY GOOD	EXCELLENT	OUTSTANDING	CURRENT	% EARNED
Client Satisfaction Score							
Level	87	91	95	99	100	99	
Bonus	0.00	1.00	2.00	3.00	4.00		3.00
Percent Staff Utilization							
Level	93	95	97	99	100	93	
Bonus	0.00	0.50	1.00	1.50	2.00		0.00%
Percent Service Deliver Cost to Budget							
Level	110	99	95	61	89	95	
Bonus	0.00	0.50	1.00	1.50	2.00		1.00%
Percent On-Time Delivery							
Level	93	95	97	99	100	97	
Bonus	0.00	1.00	2.00	3.00	4.00		2.00%
					BONUS PERCENT EARNED		6.00%

4

The Involvement System

In this chapter, we discuss one type of employee involvement system that has been proven to work well with gainsharing incentives in a variety of settings, both in manufacturing and in service organizations. For more information about employee involvement and optional involvement systems that will work with gainsharing, see Boyett & Conn, *Maximum Performance Management*, pages 253-283; Boyett & Conn, *Workplace 2000*, pages 234-265; and Boyett & Boyett, *Guru Guide*, pages 128-173.

The involvement system we recommend for gainsharing addresses the problems associated with traditional approaches such as surveys, suggestion systems, or quality circles. This involvement system is non-voluntary, is directed by line management, is an integral part of running the business, involves every employee in problem-solving activities, and provides for the creation of short-term task forces to address cross-functional problems as needed. The approach calls for the creation of work group teams that follow the traditional organizational hierarchy. Here is how the system works.

Employees in each division, department, shift, and so on are members of a work group team. There are teams at the senior management level, middle management level, supervisory level, and hourly/worker level. The leader of each team is the supervisor or manager of that particular work group. Team members are the employees who report directly to that leader.

Membership in these teams is not voluntary. Everyone in the organization, regardless of title or level, is a member of a team and receives training in problem-solving skills. All team leaders receive training in team building and leadership skills. Supervisors and middle managers are involved in two teams. They lead the team consisting of the people reporting directly to them, and they are also members of their boss's team. Any new employee automatically becomes a member of his/her boss's team.

Since the leader of each team is a manager or supervisor, every team receives direction from management. In addition, since teams follow the traditional organizational pyramid, team activity is always on line and an integral part of running the business. The involvement system is not a special program.

Involvement teams look much like the traditional organization. In fact, because they follow traditional organizational lines, they can be installed with little disruption to the existing structure. But, these teams differ from the traditional organization in three ways: (1) their activities center around a regular team meeting that is significantly different from normal staff meetings, (2) the supervisor's or manager's role is changed drastically, and (3) employees assume responsibilities that were traditionally reserved for managers and supervisors. Let us take a closer look at these new teams.

Team Meetings

In the traditional organization, it is not unusual for employees to meet as a group with their supervisor on a regular or special basis. Many supervisors hold weekly or monthly staff meetings. In such meetings, the manager or supervisor usually talks and employees listen. Upper-level decisions are announced, plant or company news is reported, orders are issued, mistakes are criticized, and poor performance is berated. If employees participate in the meeting at all, it is to answer questions, to report on the status of projects/activities, and occasionally to defend themselves from attack. In some instances, employees use these meetings to gripe, complain, socialize, point fingers, or dump problems on their boss. If problems are discussed, they are just discussed. There is usually little problem solving. A typical conclusion to a discussion of problems is, "I guess we have to do something about that." Of course, nothing is ever done. The same problem will surface at several consecutive meetings, will remain unresolved, and eventually will be forgotten as new and more pressing problems emerge.

Team meetings differ from traditional staff meetings in that they have both specific objectives and a specific structure. The objectives of the team meetings are as follow:

1. *To share information and ideas.* The team leaders link everyone in the company in an organized grapevine. The leader collects ideas, questions,

and concerns from team members and passes these upward to higher level teams. In addition, the leader passes down information about the goals, objectives, concerns, and priorities of higher levels.

2. *To monitor performance and provide feedback.* Each team has a clearly defined mission and measures of performance in critical areas. The team meeting as a major focal point for reviewing group performance in critical areas on a regular basis.

3. *To recognize and reinforce good performance.* The team leader and team members use the meeting to recognize and reinforce team members who are performing well and/or have contributed in some special way toward the achievement of group goals.

4. *To get everyone's input and ideas for improving performance.* A portion of each team meeting is set aside for problem identification, analysis, and the development of action plans to solve problems and make performance gains happen.

5. *To establish accountability for action.* Team meetings are used to review the status of action plans and task assignments from previous meetings. Individual team members are required to report back to the team on completion of their own task assignments.

The Standard Team Meeting Agenda

To meet these objectives, each team meeting follows a standard agenda of five parts. The following shows the order in which they generally occur in the meeting:

1. *Follow-up items.* The leader opens each meeting by responding to questions, ideas, concerns, and/or recommendations from the previous team meeting. Usually there are one or more items that the leader had agreed to discuss with higher levels. In this segment, the team leader reports back to the team members on the status of those items. After the leader is finished, individual team members who had task assignments from the previous team meeting are called upon to report on the status of those assignments.

2. *Performance feedback.* The second agenda item for a team meeting is a review of group performance on key indicators for the current period. This review usually involves display of the graphs on performance that are maintained by members of the team. The focus of discussion is on

positive and negative trends in performance over time and how those trends might affect gainsharing.

3. *Recognition and reinforcement.* During this segment, individual team members and/or the entire team is recognized and reinforced for performance improvement or goal attainment. Reinforcement is initiated by the team leader, who has identified in advance of the meeting one or more individuals to reinforce. A very important part of this segment is the reinforcement that individuals receive from their peers on the team.

4. *Problem solving and development of action plans.* Based upon its review of performance trends and of follow-up on action plans or task assignments from previous meetings, the team identifies one or more problems that deserve attention. These problems usually relate to performance on the key indicators being tracked by the group, those reviewed during the feedback segment of the meeting. Problem-solving efforts are facilitated by the team leader and involve the use of problem-solving techniques such as brainstorming, nominal group technique (NGT), cause and effect diagrams, or Pareto diagrams. At least the team leader has had formal training in the use of these problem-solving tools. The leader also has had formal training in leading problem-solving groups. The result of the problem-solving activity is the development of written action plans that specify what is to be done, who on the team are responsible for taking the action, and the target date for completion of the action. The team members based upon group consensus develop these action plans. The team leader does not dictate them. Problems of a cross-functional, cross-departmental, or cross-shift nature are referred by the team to higher-level teams for resolution or assignment to a special, cross-functional task force.

5. *News/announcements and meeting conclusion.* The final segment of the team meeting is devoted to announcements and general news of interest to team members. The team leader closes the meeting with a brief recap of the decisions that were made by the team concerning action plans and task assignments.

In summary, this method of employee involvement has the following advantages:

- Total participation is achieved in a short period of time,

- Management's ability to direct action and communicate priorities is increased,

- Individuals are given an opportunity to provide input to management and participate in problem solving,

- Managers help each other problem solve, and

- Each team's performance is reviewed at each team meeting so that team members are held accountable for team performance and the realization of gains.

Plant X—Involvement System

The employee involvement system for *Plant X* will be based on a series of interlocking team meetings. The executive vice president and his direct reports will make up one team. The department managers and their supervisors will make up another team. The supervisors and coordinators/forepersons will be a third level of teams. The forepersons and employees will be the fourth level of teams. All managers and supervisors will be members of two teams—one with their boss and peers and another with their direct reports. Each team meeting will serve as a regular forum for reviewing team performance, recognizing improvement in individual and team contributions and problem solving ways to improve performance and realize gains.

In addition to performance feedback, recognition and problem solving, the interlocking team meetings will also provide an excellent forum for communication up and down the organization that will be critical for the success of gainsharing at the *Plant X*. Recommendations and concerns from one level will automatically feed into managers' team meetings. Likewise, team meetings will provide an efficient mechanism for disseminating information down through the organization. In the case of improvement efforts that require cross-functional coordination, management may establish special cross-functional performance improvement problem solving and/or process reengineering teams.

Involvement System Training

The implementation of involvement teams usually involves scheduling and conducting a series of training and follow-up coaching sessions for managers, supervisors, and team leaders, designed to provide them with the skills they require to begin conducting team meetings. Our recommendation is that you arrange to conduct the training in half-day modules over a period of several weeks (approximately one module per week) so that you can provide individual follow-up coaching in applying the skills, module by module. Note that this follow-up is critical. Do not just deliver the training.

The exact content of the training you provide and the nature of the follow-up activity will depend upon the results of the assessment and the decisions of the steering committee. We use some or all of the modules shown on the following pages. As you review the content of these training modules, notice that they are designed to develop skills managers and supervisors will use in leading team meetings. The last two modules involve applying these skills in actual team meetings. Also, note that each module provides one or a more individual, follow-up coaching session, during which the trainer reviews skills taught in the training and helps the manager or supervisor apply these skills to a real life situation. As we have said previously, the follow-up coaching is actually more important than the formal training session, since it is through this type of coaching that managers and supervisors begin to change their behavior.

==

INVOLVEMENT TRAINING PLAN

==

Module #1:
Introduction to Performance Management

Objectives

Upon completion of this module and follow-up coaching, you will:

- Understand what you can do to motivate people;

- Apply the Antecedent-Behavior-Consequences Model (ABC Model) to analyze performance problems; and

- Use antecedents and consequences to achieve maximum performance.

Training Content

- Overview of performance management

- What motivates excellent performance?

- Explanation of the ABC Model

- How to apply the ABC Model to analyze and improve performance

- Practice in application of the ABC Model

Individual Follow-up Coaching Session

- Review training content

- Apply the ABC Model to an existing performance problem

===

Module #2:
Pinpointing and Performance Feedback

Preparation

Before conducting this training module, the trainer will review key perform-ance reports with management to identify critical measures and to collect cur-rent data for use in the training session.

Objectives

At the conclusion of this training session and the individual follow-up coaching, you will:

- Identify key performance measures;

- Pinpoint behaviors needed to improve key performance measures;

- Know how to improve current methods of giving performance feedback;

- Use performance feedback to motivate people.

Training Content

- How to pinpoint performance measures.

- How to pinpoint desired behaviors to improve performance.

- Practice in pinpointing.

- What is performance feedback?

- Benefits of feedback.

- Criteria for effective feedback.

- Assessment of current feedback systems.

- Explanation of the performance area selected by the management team.

Individual Follow-up Coaching Session

- Review training content

- Pinpoint key performance measures

- Pinpoint behaviors to improve performance measures

- Collect data on key performance measures

===

Module #3:
Graphing and Data Analysis

Objectives

Upon completion of this module and the follow-up coaching, you will:

- Design and create performance feedback graphs;

- Post feedback graphs in the work areas;

- Explain feedback graphs to employees; and

- Analyze and explain current performance trends.

Training Content

- Graphing as a tool for providing feedback

- Benefits of graphs over other feedback systems

- How to design a performance feedback graph
- How to analyze trends in performance data
- Analysis of current performance on key measures
- Group consensus on performance measures for employee feedback

Individual Follow-up Coaching Session-One or More Sessions

- Review training content on graphing and data analysis
- Design performance feedback graphs
- Post performance feedback graphs
- Explain graphs to employees

===

Module #4
Reflective Listening

Objectives

Upon completion of this training and the individual follow-up coaching, you will:

- Ask employees for ideas on how to improve performance;
- Rephrase employee concerns to make sure they are fully understood; and
- Use empathy, self-disclosure and reinforcement to encourage employees to express their ideas and concerns.

Training Content

- Self-assessment of listening habits
- The communication process
- The active listening process
- Active listening skills
  - Attending

- Prompting

- Open-ended question asking

- Rephrasing

- Using empathy statements

- Using self-disclosure statements

- Using reinforcing statements

Individual Follow-up Coaching Sessions

- Review training content

- Use listening skills to solicit ideas for improving performance

- Receive feedback on application of listening skills from consultant

===

Module #5
Reinforcement

Objectives

Upon completion of this training and the individual follow-up coaching, you will:

- Pinpoint behaviors to reinforce;

- Identify possible reinforcers; and

- Reinforce employees for good performance related to posted feedback graphs, following guidelines for effective reinforcement.

Training Content

- Definition of reinforcement

- Different types of reinforcers

- How to identify behaviors to reinforce

- How to select appropriate reinforcers

- Guidelines for effective reinforcement

- Practice in reinforcing good performance

Individual Follow-up Coaching Session

- Review training content

- Identify behaviors to reinforce related to improving performance on feedback graphs

- Select possible reinforcers for identified behaviors

- Practice reinforcing, with observation and feedback by consultant

===

Module #6
Correcting Undesirable Performance

Objectives

Upon completion of this training module and the individual follow-up coaching, you will:

- Select an appropriate model for use in correcting undesirable performance; and

- Use the selected model effectively to correct undesirable performance.

Training Content

- The difference between punishment and correcting

- Benefits of correcting

- Models for effective correcting: Empathy Model, Shaping Model, Negative Feedback Model

- When and how to use each model

- Practice in selecting and using correcting models

Individual Follow-up Coaching Session

- Review training content

- Identify undesirable performance or behavior

- Select appropriate correcting model

- Apply model and discuss results with consultant

===

Module #7
Creative Problem Solving

Objectives

Upon completion of the training and the follow-up coaching, you will:

- Apply the group problem solving skills of brainstorming, consensus decision making, and action planning to improve performance; and

- Lead groups in problem solving using these skills.

Training Content

- Discussion of current methods for employee involvement in problem identification and problem solving

- Explanation of creative problem-solving skills: brainstorming, consensus decision making, and action planning

- Application of creative problem-solving skills

- Introduction Of Creative Problem Solving Model

Individual Follow-up Coaching Session

- Review training content

- Apply creative problem-solving skills in management team meeting

- Receive feedback on application of creative problem-solving skills from consultant

===

Module #8
Effective Meetings

Objectives

Upon Completion of this training and the follow-up coaching session, you will:

- Conduct effective team meetings following the standard agenda;

- Encourage participation in a team meeting;

- Effectively handle disruptive behavior in a team meeting; and

- Use skills acquired in the previous training to conduct these meetings.

Training Content

- What makes a good meeting?

- How to prepare a team meeting agenda.

- How to prepare for a team meeting.

- How to lead a team meeting.

- How to encourage participation.

- How to handle disruptive behavior.

Individual Follow-up Coaching Session

- Review training content

- Prepare for a team meeting

===

Module #9
Team Meetings

Objectives

Upon completion of this training and the follow-up coaching, you will:

- Conduct a team meeting that using performance feedback, rein-forcement, problem solving, and communication.

Training Content

Mock team meetings are used to illustrate the process and development of team meetings over time. Participants refine their skills in conducting team meetings in a variety of situations.

Individual Follow-up Coaching Session

- Prepare to lead a team meeting;

- Conduct a team meeting and receive feedback on team leadership skills from consultant.

==

Module #10
Advanced Creative Problem Solving

Objectives

Upon completion of this training and the follow-up coaching, you will:

- Apply creative problem-solving skills to define a problem,

- Analyze potential causes of the problem,

- Develop alternative solutions,

- Select among alternative solutions, and

- Implement solutions.

Training Content

Review steps involved in the Creative Problem-Solving Model: problem identification and definition; problem analysis using cause and effect diagrams, check sheets, and Pareto diagrams; development of solutions; and implementation and follow up.

Individual Follow-up Coaching

- Review training content.

- Use Creative Problem-Solving Model and skills in team meetings.

- Receive feedback on application of Creative Problem-Solving Model and skills from consultant.

5

Implementing and Maintaining

After the task force has completed the gainsharing document, it should be reviewed by company attorneys and then submitted to senior management for approval. However, before you submit the document for legal review and executive approval, the task force should conduct one final review of the gainsharing plan. First, revisit the "Keys to Success" we discussed earlier. Have you covered all of these in your design document? Second, the task force should discuss and agree upon answers to the ten questions in Exhibit 5.1. If there is not one hundred percent agreement among the members of the ask force that the truthfully answer to each of these questions is YES, your plan may contain significant flaws.

Exhibit 5.1
Gainsharing Task Force
Gainsharing Plan Final Review

	QUESTIONS	YES	NO
1.	Can the people who will be participating in the plan influence the performance measured by the gainsharing formula in a significant way by changes in their day-to-day behavior? Very little if any of the variation in performance should be due to factors outside of the control of the gainsharing plan participants.		
2.	Will the participants understand the connection between their day-to-day behavior on the job and the results on the performance indicators used in the gainsharing formula? In other words, will they see a direct connection between what they do and the results as measured by the gainsharing formula? If not, how will you train them to see the connection?		
3.	If the gainsharing targets are met and exceeded, will the organization as a whole benefit in both the short and long term? Are you sure there is no downside for the organization if the gainsharing targets are met and people earn substantial bonuses?		
4.	Will the gainsharing participants see the gainsharing targets as challenging but legitimate and attainable? Targets should be specific and difficult but reasonable and justifiable given historical performance, the business strategy and the competitive environment. Targets should not be arbitrary.		
5.	If multiple measures of performance are used in the gainsharing formula, have they been weighted in some way to reflect their relative importance for the short-term and long-term health of the organization?		
6.	Will gainsharing participants receive specific, frequent, objective and clearly understandable feedback on performance against the gainsharing target? Will the feedback relate to their specific behavior and not just performance outcomes? In other words, will the feedback be useful in providing guidance to the participants concerning how they need to change their behavior(s) to realize gainsharing payouts?		
7.	Will gainsharing participants have an effective mechanism for initiating changes in work procedures and methods and/or requesting new or additional resources such as new technology they may feel they need to improve performance and realize gains? While management must control the allocation of resources, gainsharing participants have a right to expect that management will agree to reasonable and justifiable requests for additional resources and/or changes in work methods.		
8.	If the work of multiple groups, departments, or divisions will influence performance measured by the gainsharing formula is there an effective mechanism for coordinating the efforts of the multiple groups involved and insuring high levels of communication, information sharing, and cooperation?		
9.	Are other social and/or financial reward programs, currently in existence or planned, consistent with the gainsharing program? For example, are managerial and supervisory bonus/incentive programs consistent with the gainsharing plan? Are existing social award and recognition programs such as "employee of the month" or suggestion awards, consistent with the gainsharing plan?		
10.	Does the culture of the group, department, and/or organization as a whole support employee involvement, empowerment, and the participation of employees in decision-making? Will most employees be willing to take some financial risk and accept greater responsibilities in return for financial rewards and greater control over their work life? Will the owners/managers of the business be willing to give up some control over the way work is performed in order to gain greater employee commitment and the benefit of their ideas? Will the owners/managers of the business be willing to share the financial gains that come from employee efforts even if the gainsharing bonuses turn out to be substantial—10%, 20%, or even more?		

Implementation

After the task force has completed the gainsharing document, it should be reviewed by company attorneys and then submitted to senior management for approval. Once approved, the implementation process begins. Two steps are critical to implementation: (1) securing employee acceptance and approval, and (2) initiating employee involvement efforts.

To secure employee approval, the task force should initiate information programs to familiarize managers, supervisors, and employees with the specifics of the plan. The plan should be discussed at a kick off meeting during which employees should be provided with a summary of key features of the plan plus examples of test calculations. (See Exhibit 5.2 for a sample agenda for a kick off meeting.) In particular, efforts should be made to explain the productivity-sharing emphasis in the plan—how everyone can win—and to dispel any fears employees might have that the formula will be manipulated by management to benefit the company unfairly. You may want to conduct an employee survey after the kick off meeting to determine how well the communication effort has worked. You may want to have employees and managers/supervisors vote on whether to implement the gainsharing plan. Whether you have a vote or simply conduct a survey, we do not recommend that you proceed with gainsharing unless at least 80 percent of managers, supervisors and employees approve.

Equally important to the introduction of the plan is the initiation of employee involvement projects. Ideally, the involvement program will have progressed to a point that employee problem-solving meetings are already being conducted on a regular basis and some projects are already underway. It is particularly important that these improvement efforts be tied into gainsharing.

Exhibit 5.2

GAINSHARING KICK OFF MEETING AGENDA

NOTE: You may need to hold more than one meeting to accommodate all employees, managers, and supervisors.

TIMING

The meeting should be held at least one week
before plan implementation.

ATTENDEES

Corporate representative(s), plant/group manager,
and all participants

SEATING

Attendees should be seated by team or group
8 to 12 people per group.

HANDOUTS

Copy of plan or employee summary. Sample calculations.

AGENDA

TIME	Activity	Process	WHO
00:00-00:05	Introduction	Welcome participants. Review the agenda. Explain team discussions and how the open forum will work.	Plant Manager
00:05-00:15	Corporate Perspective	Corporate goals for plant. Why plant was chosen for pilot. Expression of support for incentive plan.	Corporate Representative
00:15-00:20	Plan Objectives	Review of plan objectives. Why are we doing this?	Plant Manager
00:20-00:45	Administrative Provisions	Explanation of administrative provisions: Participant Group Eligibility Requirements Allocation Basis Performance Period Holdback Provision Sunset Provision Adjustment Provision Buyback Provision Bonus Ceiling Sharing Ratio	Plant Personnel Manager, HR manager or other manager.
00:45-01:00	Review of Formula	Review of formula calculation. Review of sample "what if" calculations	Plant Manager
01:00-01:15	Group Discussion	In their groups, attendees discuss the following: What were our reactions to this plan? What questions do we have about the plan that, if answered, would help us to better understand how the plan will work? Groups pick a spokesperson and agree upon three to five questions they would like to ask as a group.	Participants working in small groups.
00:15-01:55	Open Forum	Groups are called upon one at a time to ask their questions. Managers answer questions. Questions are restricted to understanding questions only—no speeches!	Plant Manager serves as Moderator
00:55-02:00	Closing	Participants are invited to raise any additional questions individually with plant managers or in their regular team meetings.	Plant Manager

Evaluation

Particularly during the first year, the gainsharing program must be monitored closely. The gainsharing task force should meet on a regular basis to review these and other issues:

1.   Do managers, supervisors, and employees understand the plan?

2.   Are improvement projects being initiated?

3.   Are improvements resulting from the implementation of employee ideas?

4.   Are bonuses being paid?

5.   Has company performance improved?

6.   Are changes required in the gainsharing plan?

The result of this year-long evaluation should be a recommendation from the task force at the end of the year concerning whether or not the program should be retained, and if retained, whether modifications are necessary. A formal, year-end review and another employee survey is appropriate to ensure that the program continues to meet the needs and objectives of both employees and the company. In fact, the sunshine provision requires a formal review of the plan after the first year and provides that the plan will lapse unless a specific decision is made to continue.

See Exhibit 5.3 for a list of questions you can use to troubleshoot problems with your gainsharing plan.

Exhibit 5.3
Troubleshooting Gainsharing
The 20 Keys to Success

If your gainsharing program is not producing the results you desire, here are some questions to ask that may help you pinpoint where your program went wrong and what you can do to improve.

	QUESTION	YES	NO
1.	Did you build a business case for gainsharing? Did you align the program and rewards with the business strategy? Does gainsharing support your business objectives?		
2.	Did you implement gainsharing in a capital-intensive organization? Gainsharing has been shown to be most successful in labor-intensive organizations where employees can significantly affect performance outcomes thorough their ideas and actions.		
3.	Did you implement gainsharing during a time of financial crisis or when the business did not have the funds to invest in program administration and employee development and training?		
4.	Did you rely to heavily upon outside consultants? Managers and employees must design the gainsharing plan themselves in order to develop a sense of ownership of the plan and to acquire the skills to be able to maintain and revise the plan over time.		
5.	Did you design the plan in isolation without adequate input from managers, supervisors, team leaders, the union and employees?. Gainsharing plans designed by outside consultants or a single or small group of managers without employee and/or union input are doomed to failure.		
6.	Did you spend an adequate amount of time designing the gainsharing plan? You should spend from six to nine months designing the gainsharing plan. It takes that amount of time to work through all of the issues and to gain commitment to the plan. Plans that are designed in haste quickly fail.		
7.	Did you involve the union early on in the gainsharing design process? You must gain union support or at least acquiescence to gainsharing or your plan cannot succeed.		
8.	Did you involve employees in the decision to undertake gainsharing and in the design process? Consider having employees vote on the plan and do not proceed unless 80 percent of employees approve.		
9.	Did you keep the gainsharing participant group relatively small? The number of participants covered by a single gainsharing plan should be less than 500 and preferably less than 200.		
10.	Did you keep the plan simple and easy to understand? Did you the formula contain only items that were controllable by plan participants?		
11.	Were the gainsharing targets reasonable and justifiable given historical trends and competitive requirements? Were the targets seen as fair and reasonable by employees and managers alike?		
12.	Was the potential for gains sufficient to produce average bonus payments of $100 per month per employee? Ideally, employees should have to potential of earning average bonuses of $200 per month or more. Research suggests that it takes bonuses, or at least the potential for bonuses, of $100 per month to get employees' attention and $200 per month to get them excited.		
13.	Did you calculate and pay gainsharing bonuses monthly or weekly rather than quarterly or annually? Employees will see a greater connection between their efforts and gainsharing bonuses if the bonuses are paid close to the time of the performance that led to the gain.		

	QUESTION	YES	NO
14.	Did you attempt to implement gainsharing without strong support from the senior executives of the organization and the majority of managers and supervisors? The senior manager of the organization implementing gainsharing should be prepared to state his/her commitment to the philosophy of gainsharing and the organization's gainsharing plan both verbally and in writing prior to the implementation of the plan.		
15.	Was a structured system of employee involvement such as employee teams or a suggestion system in place and operational BEFORE the start of gainsharing? Were employees and managers fully trained in the operation of the involvement system?		
16.	Did employees understand the drivers of the gainsharing formula and how they could affect the potential for gains by changes in their behavior? There should be a direct "line-of-sight" between employee behavior and gainsharing results.		
17.	Did you invest heavily in employee training and re-training to ensure that employees understood the gainsharing plan and had the problem-solving and other skills necessary to find ways to make gains happen?		
18.	Did you make extensive use of banners, meetings, bulletin boards, newsletters and other communication devices to keep employees informed about the status of the gainsharing program during the design process and once the program was implemented? Did you do an adequate job of communicating with employees about the gainsharing plan and how to make gains happen?		
19.	Did you implement the gainsharing plan when business conditions were good and there was the potential to realize early gains? Did the organization realize early gains? If not, why not?		
20.	Do you conduct regularly scheduled formal reviews of the gainsharing plan (at least annually) to make sure the plan is working for employees, the company and other stakeholders? Have you revise the plan as necessary based upon what you have learned?		

Gainsharing Resources

Books and Articles

Arthur, Jeffrey B. and Lynda Airman-Smith, "Gainsharing and Organizational Learning: An Analysis of Employee Suggestions Over Time," *Academy of Management Journal*, August 2001, Volume 44, Issue 4, p. 737-754.

Arthur, Jeffrey B. and Gregory S. Jeff, "The Effects of Gainsharing on Grievance Rates and Absenteeism Over Time," *Journal of Labor* Research, Winter 1999, p. 133-145

Belcher, John G., Jr., *How to Design & Implement a Results-Oriented Variable Pay System*, AMACOM, 1996. ISBN 0-814-40296-8

Boyett, Joseph H. and Henry P. Conn, *Maximum Performance Management: How to Manage and Compensate People to Meet World Competition*, Glenbridge Publishing Ltd., 1988. ISBN 0-944435-03-3.

Boyett, Joseph H. and Henry P. Conn, *Workplace 2000: The Revolution Reshaping American Business*, Dutton/ Penguin USA, 1991. ISBN 0-525-24936-2.

Boyett, Joseph H. and Jimmie T. Boyett. *Beyond Workplace 2000: Essential Strategies for the New American Corporation*, Dutton, 1995. ISBN 0-525-93782-X.

Boyett, Joseph H. and Jimmie T. Boyett. *The Guru Guide: The Best Ideas of the Top Management Thinkers*, John Wiley & Sons, Inc., 1998. ISBN 0-471-18242-7.

Boyett, Joseph H. and Henry P. Conn, "Pay-for-Knowledge: How to Increase Employee Flexibility," *Brief 68, American Productivity & Quality Center*. November 1988.

Bullock, R. J. and Patti F. Bullock, "Gainsharing and Rubik's Cube: Solving System Problems," *National Productivity Review*, Autumn 1982, p. 396-407.

Bullock, R. J. and E.E. Lawler, "Gainsharing: A Few Questions and Fewer Answers," *Human Resource Management* 1984, Volume 23, Number 1, p. 23-40.

Bullock, R. J. and M. E. Tubbs, "A Case Meta-Analysis of Gainsharing Plans as Organization Development Interventions," *Journal of Applied Behavioral Science*, 1990, Volume 23, Number 3, p. 383-404.

Cahill, Noel. *Profit Sharing, Employee Share Ownership and Gainsharing: What Can They Achieve?* National Economic and Social Council, Research Series No. 4, May 2000.

Collins, Denis, "Case Study: 15 Lessons Learned from the Death of a Gainsharing Plan," *Compensation and Benefits Review*, March/April 1996, Volume 28, Number 2, p.31-40.

Collins, Denis. *Gainsharing and Power: Lessons from Six Scanlon Plans*, Cornell University Press, 1998. ISBN 0-801-43490-4

Collins, D., L. Hatcher, and T. L. Ross, "The Decision to Implement Gainsharing: The Role of Work Climate, Expected Outcomes and Union Status," *Personnel Psychology*, 1993, Volume 46, Number 1, p. 77-105.

Cooper, Christine L., Bruno Dyck, and Norman Frohlich, "Improving the Effectiveness of Gainsharing: The Role of Fairness and Participation," *Administrative Science Quarterly*, 37 (1992) p. 471-490.

Cox, Annette, "The Importance of Employee Participation in Determining Pay System Effectiveness," *International Journal of Management Reviews*, December 2000, Volume 2, Issue 4, p. 357-376.

Dalton, Glenn, "Electromation's Aftermath: Weighing the Legal Risks and Rewards of Employee Involvement Programs," *Compensation & Benefits Review*, July 7, 1996, Volume 28, p. 14-23.

Daniels, Aubrey, *Bringing Out the Best in People*, McGraw-Hill, 1994. ISBN 0-07-015358-2.

Doherty, E.M., W. R. Nord, and J.L. McAdams, "Gainsharing and Organization Development: A Productive Synergy," *Journal of Applied Behavioral Science*, 1989, Volume 25, Number 3, p. 209-229.

Ehrenfeld, Tom, "The Productivity-Boosting Gain-Sharing Report," *INC*, August 1991, p. 87-89.

Fein, Mitchell, *Improshare: An Alternative to Traditional Managing*, American Institute of Industrial Engineers, 1981. ISBN: 0-89806-031-1.

Feuer, Dale, "Paying for Knowledge," *Training*, May 1987, p. 57-65.

Franklin, Jerry, "For Technical Professionals: Pay for Skills and Pay for Performance," *Personnel*, May 1988, p. 20-28.

Garvey, Charlotte, "Goalsharing Scores," *HRMagazine*, April 2000, p. 99-106.

Giblin, Edward J. and Leslie G. Kelley, "Three Self-destructive Pay Mistakes," *Across the Board*, May 1994, p. 40-43.

Gomez-Mejia, Luis R., Thresa M. Welbourne, and Robert M. Wiseman, "The Role of Risk Sharing and Risk Taking Under Gainsharing," *Academy of Management Review*, Vol. 25, No.3, 2000, p. 492-507.

Gowen, C.R., "Gainsharing Programs: An Overview of History and Research," *Journal of Organizational Behavior Management*, 1991, Volume 11, Number 2, p. 77-99.

Graham-Moore, Brian and Timothy L. Ross, *Gainsharing and Employee Involvement*, Bureau of National Affairs, Inc., 1995. ISBN 0-871-79875-1

Gupta, Nina, G. Douglas Jenkins, and William P. Curington, "Paying for Knowledge: Myths and Realities," *National Productivity Review*, Spring 1986, p. 107-123.

Gupta, Nina, Thmothy P. Schweizer, and G. Douglas Jenkins, Jr., "Pay-for-Knowledge compensation plans: hypotheses and survey results," *Monthly Labor Review*, October 1987, p. 40-43.

Hanlon, S.C. and D.G. Meyer, "Consequences of Gainsharing," *Group and Organization Management*, 1994, Volume 19, Number 1, p. 87-112.

Hauck, Warren C., "Productivity Gainsharing: Is It Applicable to Service Sector Firms?," *Industrial Management*, July-August 1982, p. 164-169.

Hochwarter, Wayne A., "When to Use and When Not to Use Gainsharing Programs," *Supervision*, June 1995, p. 8-11.

Imberman, Woodruff, "Gainsharing: A Lemon or Lemonade," *Business Horizons*, January/February 1996, Volume 39, Issue 1, p. 36-41.

IOMA, "Goalsharing or Gainsharing: Which is Better for You?," *IOMA's Pay for Performance Report,* November 2000, Issue 00-11, p. 1-15.

IOMA, "Scanlon & Skill: Two Compensation Plans for These Difficult Times," *IOMA's Pay for Performance Report,* December 2002, Issue 02-12, p. 1-12.

Kanter, Rosabeth Moss, "From Status to Contribution: Some Organizational Implications of the Changing Basis of Pay," *Personnel,* January 1987, p. 12-37.

Kaufman, R. T., "The Effects of IMPROSHARE on Productivity," *Industrial and Labor Relations Review,* 1992, Volume 45, Number 2, p. 311-322.

Kay, Ira T. and Diane Lerner, "What's Good for the Parts May Hurt the Whole," *HRMagazine,* Summer 1995, p. 71-77.

Kim, Dong-One, "Determinants of the Survival of Gainsharing Programs," *Industrial & Labor Relations Review,* October 1999, p. 21-42.

Kim, Dong-One, "Factors Influencing Organizational Performance in Gainsharing Programs," *Industrial Relations,* 1996, Volume 35, Number 2, p. 227-244.

Kim, Dong-One and P.B. Voos, "Unionization, Union Involvement, and the Performance of Gainsharing Programs," *Relations Industrielles /Industrial Relations,* 1997, Volume 52, Number 2, p. 304-332.

Lienert, Anita, "A Dinosaur of a Different Color," *Management Review,* February 1995, p.24-29.

Luthans, Fred and Marilyn L. Fox, "Update on Skill-Based Pay," *Personnel,* March 1989, p. 26-31.

Mangel, Robert, "The Strategic Role of Gainshairing," *Journal of Labor Research,* Spring 2000, Volume 21, Number 2, p. 327-343.

Markham, S.E., K.D. Scott, and B.L. Little, "National Gainsharing Study: The Importance of Industry Differences," *Compensation & Benefits Review,* August 1992, p. 36-40.

Masternak, Robert L., "How to Make Gainsharing Successful: The Collective Experience of 17 Facilities," *Compensation and Benefits Review,* September/October 1997, p. 43-52.

Masternak, Robert L., "Gainsharing: Overcoming Common Myths and Problems to Achieve Dramatic Results," *Employment Relations Today*, Winter 1993/94, p. 425-436.

McGrath, Thomas C., "How Three Screw Machine Companies are Tapping Human Productivity Through Gainsharing," *Employment Relations Today*, Winter 1993/94, p. 43746.

Mericle, Kenneth and Dong-One Kim, *Gainsharing and Goalsharing: Aligning Pay and Strategic Goals*, Praeger, 2004. ISBN: 1-56720-492-9.

Mericle, Ken and John Lund, "Variable Compensation Plans, Overtime Calculations, and the Fair Labor Standards Act," *Labor Law Review*, August 1995, p. 492-503.

Morris, John L., "Bonus Dollars for Team Players," *HRMagazine*, February 1995, p. 7683.

Musselwhite, W. Christopher, "Knowledge, Pay, and Performance," *Training and Development Journal*, January 1988, p. 62-65.

Nalbantian, H.R. and A. Schotter, "Productivity Under Group Incentives: An Experimental Study," *American Economic Review*, 1997, Volume 87, Number 3, p. 314-341.

Novak, C. James, "Proceed with Caution When Paying Teams," *HR Magazine*, April 1997, Vol. 42, Issue 4, p. 73-77,

O'Bannon, Douglas P., "An Exploratory Examination of Gainsharing in Service Organizations: Implications for Organizational Citizenship Behavior and Pay Satisfaction," *Journal of Managerial Issues*, Fall 1999, p. 363-378.

O'Dell, Carla S. *Gainsharing: Involvement, Incentives, and Productivity*, AMACOM, AMA Management Briefing, 1981. ISBN: 0-8144-2255-1.

O'Neill, Darlene, "Blending the best of profit sharing and gainsharing," *HRMagazine*, March 1994, p. 66-70.

Overman, Stephenie, "No-frills HR at Nucor," *HRMagazine*, July 1994, p. 56-60.

Poole, Jeanne, William F. Rathgeber III, and Stanley W. Silverman, "Paying for Performance in a TQM Environment," *HRMagazine* October 1993, p. 68-73.

Recardo, Ronald and Diane Pricone, "How to Determine Whether Gainsharing is Right for You," *Industrial Management*, January/February 1996, Volume 38, Issue 1, p. 12-19.

Ringham, Arthur J., "Designing a Gainsharing Program to Fit a Company's Operations," *National Productivity Review*, Spring 1984, p. 131-144.

Ross, Timothy L. and Ruth Ann Ross, "Productivity Gainsharing: Resolving Some of the Measurement Issues," *National Productivity Review*, Autumn 1984, p. 382-394.

Schmid, R.O., "Structuring Gainsharing for Success," *Industrial Engineering*, July 1994, p. 62-65.

Schuster, Michael, "Gain Sharing: Do It Right the First Time," *Sloan Management Review*, Winter 1987, p. 17-25.

Sheehy, Barry and Gordon Peckover, "You Get What You Pay For," *Industrial Management*, September 1988, p. 25-26.

Stenhouse, Thomasina R., "The Long and the Short of Gainsharing," *The Academy of Management Executive*, 1995, Vol. 9, No. 1, p. 77-78.

Thomas, B. W. and M. H. Olson, "Gainsharing: The Design Guarantees Success," *Personnel Journal*, 1988, Volume 67, Number 5, 73-79.

Timmins, William J., "Team-Based Compensation at Recently Reengineered Zeneca Ag Products," *Employment Relations Today*, Summer 1995, p. 43-51.

Verespej, Michael A., "New Responsibilities? New Pay!," *Industry Week*, August 15, 1994, p. 11-22.

Welbourne, Theresa M. and Luis R. Gomaz Mejia, "Gainsharing: A Critical Review and a Future Research Agenda," *Journal of Management* 1995, Vol 21, No. 3, p. 559-609.

White, J.K., "The Scanlon Plan: Causes and Correlates of Success," *Academy of Management Journal*, 1979, Volume 22, Number 2, p. 292-312.

Woika, Michael, "Pay Plan Based on Performance Motivates Employees," *HRMagazine* December 1993, p. 75-77.

Zamora, Gloria, "How Whirlpool Corporation Uses Varied Performance-Based Compensation Programs to Achieve Strategic Ends," *Employment Relations Today*, Spring 1994, p. 45-54.

Web Sites

Scanlon Leadership Network

Non-profit association promoting Scanlon-type gainsharing. http://www.scanlonleader.org. Provides news, resources, educational materials, best practices, access to membership network, certified consultants, etc. See their "Links" page for links to web sites of members of the Scanlon Leadership Network who have implemented Scanlon-type gainsharing.

Scanlon Leadership Network
2875 Northwind Drive, Suite 121
East Lansing, MI 48823
(517) 332-8927

Boyett & Associates

Our web site at http://www.jboyett.com provides articles and additional information on gainsharing, skill-based pay and participative management practices. The site is periodically updated with new findings and articles.

Boyett & Associates
125 Stepping Stone Lane
Alpharetta, GA 30004-4009
(770) 667-9904

Forms

Please feel free to copy and reproduce the forms contained in this section of *The Gainsharing Design Workbook* for use in designing your gainsharing plan.

Joseph H. Boyett, Ph.D.
Jimmie T. Boyett
Boyett & Associates

Is Gainsharing Right for You?

	Question	Yes	No
1.	Does the organization in which you intend to implement gainsharing have fewer than 500 employees? [Note: Gainsharing can work with groups of up to 2,000, but is most successful when the participating group is smaller.]		
2.	Is the culture of the organization egalitarian and participative? Do managers emphasize commitment over control?		
3.	Do you have in place or are you willing to develop management systems that support open commun- ication / sharing of financial and operating inform- ation with employees?		
4.	Is there a strong and compelling need for the organization to improve performance that justifies the kind of extensive change in workplace practices the gainsharing entails? Can you easily justify the sacrifices people will have to make in order to implement gainsharing?		
5.	Are at least 75% of senior managers at the site willing to support the implementation of gainsharing publicly and privately? Are they willing and able to commit financial and other resources under their control to the success of the gainsharing effort?		
6.	Is there at least one true champion of gainsharing at the site whose opinion is respected by other managers and employees and who is willing to use his/her influence and control over key resources (money, people, technology, etc.) to support gainsharing?		
7.	Is there at least one true champion of gainsharing at the corporate level whose opinion is respected by other managers and employees and who is willing to use his/her influence and control over key resources (money, people, technology, etc.) to support gainsharing?		
8.	Is there at least one person with experience or formal training in gainsharing on site who can be designated as the full-time gainsharing coordinator (½ time for sites with fewer than 200 employees) during a six-month to one-year implementation? If yes, who is that person? Name:_____		
9.	Are the following functional areas/departments considered to be effective, efficient, flexible, and trusted by employees, and are they able to communicate effectively with employees: [Note: Each of these will be called upon to support gainsharing.]		
	Engineering		
	Maintenance		
	Purchasing		
	Scheduling		
	Quality Assurance		
	Personnel/Human Resources		
	Accounting		
10.	Do the technology and work processes at the location to be covered by gainsharing require/benefit from employee information sharing, teamwork, and cooperation?		
11.	Is accurate financial information (data on revenues, costs, etc.) available for the site for at least three to five years?		

	Question	Yes	No
12.	Is accurate operating data (productivity, quality, customer satisfaction, throughput time, and so on) available for the site for at least the last three to five years?		
13.	If productivity improved as a result of gainsharing, is there sufficient market for the increased product and/or work that could be shifted to the site to absorb the increased capacity?		
14.	Are the product/service lines relatively stable? [Note: It is probably not wise to install gainsharing at the same time you are undergoing a major change in product/service lines.]		
15.	Is the site free from significant seasonal fluctuations in demand?		
16.	Are major capital investments planned for the site in the near future that might significantly change the labor input required to produce the product or service?		
17.	Is employee job satisfaction at the site relatively high?		
18.	Do employees trust site managers?		
19.	Are labor/management relations at the site positive?		
20.	If there is a union, is the union supportive or at least neutral when it comes to gainsharing?		

Assessing the Feasibility of Gainsharing

Strategic Direction

How would gainsharing strengthen the organization's planned strategic direction?

Top Management Attitude

What is the attitude of top management at your location toward participative management and gainsharing?

Potential for Gains

Which area(s) of performance should be the focus of the gainsharing effort?

What is the potential for improvement in these areas?

Organizational dependencies

Are performance gains dependent upon cooperation and teamwork? If so, how?

Organizational Climate

What is the current state of management/employee relations?

Areas of Concern	Strength/ Positive	Weakness/ Negative	Required Action
Knowledge of and reaction to gainsharing.			
Knowledge of company strategic direction and departmental/ unit mission.			
Nature of and reaction to organizational change that has occurred in the last few years, such as changes in management, work methods, technology, etc.			
Top down communication.			
Communication across functions and shifts.			
Use of supervisor and employee meetings, and what happens in these meetings.			
Existence of operational goals and objectives-do they exist at every level, are they understood, how are they set, are they viewed as fair and reasonable?			
Existence of measurements and feedback systems.			
Use of social reinforcement.			
Use of performance appraisals—Do they exist, how are they done, how helpful are they?			

Areas of Concern	Strength/ Positive	Weakness/ Negative	Required Action
Decision-making/problem-solving styles and existence of/reaction to any employee involvement programs.			
Existence of incentive plans (including group, individual, etc.).			
Ideas for improvement-manager, supervisor, and employee evaluations of key areas for focus under gainsharing. Also, their assessment of the potential for gains through changes in employee behavior.			
Job satisfaction-morale, trust, and management/employee relations.			

Recommendation of the Task Force

Based on the answers to the questions above, what is the recommendation of the gainsharing task force?

Gainsharing should be implemented immediately.

Implementation of gainsharing should be postponed until the following actions have been taken. (Include a list of actions.)

Gainsharing Task Force Membership

List below those individuals who should serve on the gainsharing task force. Task force members should include: a senior manager, the location manager, the comptroller, the personnel or human resources manager, functional area managers, a union steward (if there is a union involved) and, optionally, employee representatives. The task force should not exceed 20 members.

Proposed Task Force Members

NAME	TITLE

Employee Representatives (optional)

Implementation Timeline

Week Ending	Activity	Participants

Objectives for the Gainsharing Program

List below your objectives for the gainsharing program. Consider all relevant interests in the program, including those of managers, employees, stockholders and customers, and assure that your objectives can be supported by each of these groups. Also, provide some direction as to how these objectives should be attained.

Participant Group

Define your participant group below, taking into consideration the interdependence of various groups and who could contribute to possible gains. Ideally, your participant group will number less than 500 employees.

Eligibility Requirements

Define the eligibility requirements for your participant group below. Eligibility refers to the requirements that must be met by members of the participant group before they can receive bonus payments. For example, normally there is a provision that new hires must complete a specified number of days of employment before being eligible for gainsharing bonuses. Additionally, decide what effect, if any, unexcused absences, personal leave, sick leave, etc. should have on eligibility for bonuses or what effect such events will have on how bonuses hare calculated. As a rule, employees should be eligible as soon as they contribute to gains.

Allocation Basis

Describe the allocation basis chosen for your gainsharing plan. Include descriptions of the method of allocation (part of paychecks or separate check), payout period and your choice of allocation method (equal shared, hours worked, or percent of total income). Keep in mind that percent of total income is the only method that ensures compliance under the Fair Labor Standards Act.

Performance Period

The performance period refers to the time period over which gains are calculated and the amount of time allowed for calculating payments due and issuing checks. Describe below the performance period selected for your plan.

Holdback Provision

Should a portion of the employee bonus be held back until the end of the year to protect the company against temporary spikes in performance?

YES [   ]   NO [   ]

If your answer is Yes:

What percentage will be held back? [   ]%

What will happen to the funds that are held back?

```
_____
_____
_____
_____
_____
```

Should the holdback be allowed to go negative?

YES [   ]   NO [   ]

If Yes, then what happens if the holdback becomes negative?

```
_____
_____
_____
_____
```

4. Who is eligible to receive holdback payments?

Sunset Provision

Is there a Sunset date when the gainsharing plan will be formally reviewed to determine whether to retain, revise or discontinue the plan?

YES [   ]   NO [   ]

If the answer is Yes, what is that date? _____

Will an employee survey be conducted?

YES [   ]   NO [   ]

If Yes, what will the date of the survey be?

_____

B. Who will prepare and administer the survey?

Name: _____

Title: _____

C. How will the results of the survey be shared with employees?

1. In team meetings. [ ]

2. In a special organization-wide meeting. [ ]

3. Other. (Specify)

_____

Adjustment Provision for Management-Initiated Changes

What provisions should be made for changes that might occur in the way business is conducted? Consider such occurrences as changes in the company's products or services, major capital investments, and the introduction of new technology.

Buyback Provision

Does the company opt to retain the right to buy back a change in the base from which gains are calculated by making a one-time payment to employees?

YES [   ]   NO [   ]

If your answer is Yes, describe the circumstances under which the company may exercise the buyback provision and at what percentage the company will buy back the base change.

Bonus Ceiling

Should there be a ceiling on how much bonus employees can earn?

YES [ ]   NO [ ]

If yes, what is the maximum percentage an employee can earn?

[ ]%

What will happen to gains earned in excess of the cap?

Sharing Ratio

Describe the ratio at which the company and employees will share the savings achieved through gainsharing. A 50/50 split is preferable, but other ratios (60/40, 75/25, etc.) are possible. Include a justification for your choice.

Gainsharing Formula

Detail your organization's consensus on a gainsharing formula. Provide several examples of gainsharing calculations, using historical data and what-if scenarios.

Administrative Details

What kind of first-year adjustments will there be to the gainsharing program?

Who will absorb training costs associated with gainsharing?

How will employees be transitioned from any individual incentive to gainsharing?

Involvement System

Discuss what type of involvement system you will use and what type of training/coaching you will provide managers, supervisors and employees in how to run this involvement system.

_____

_____

_____

_____

_____

_____

_____

_____

_____

_____

_____

_____

_____

_____

_____

_____

_____

_____

_____

Involvement System Training Plan

Describe your involvement system training plan, including the objectives and content of each training session. You should also identify the trainers and attendees for each session.

Gainsharing Plan Final Review

	QUESTIONS	YES	NO
1.	Can the people who will be participating in the plan influence the performance measured by the gainsharing formula in a significant way by changes in their day-to-day behavior? Very little if any of the variation in performance should be due to factors outside of the control of the gainsharing plan participants.		
2.	Will the participants understand the connection between their day-to-day behavior on the job and the results on the performance indicators used in the gainsharing formula? In other words, will they see a direct connection between what they do and the results as measured by the gainsharing formula? If not, how will you train them to see the connection?		
3.	If the gainsharing targets are met and exceeded, will the organization as a whole benefit in both the short and long term? Are you sure there is no downside for the organization if the gainsharing targets are met and people earn substantial bonuses?		
4.	Will the gainsharing participants see the gainsharing targets as challenging but legitimate and attainable? Targets should be specific and difficult but reasonable and justifiable given historical performance, the business strategy and the competitive environment. Targets should not be arbitrary.		
5.	If multiple measures of performance are used in the gainsharing formula, have they been weighted in some way to reflect their relative importance for the short-term and long-term health of the organization?		
6.	Will gainsharing participants receive specific, frequent, objective and clearly understandable feedback on performance against the gainsharing target? Will the feedback relate to their specific behavior and not just performance outcomes? In other words, will the feedback be useful in providing guidance to the participants concerning how they need to change their behavior(s) to realize gainsharing payouts?		
7.	Will gainsharing participants have an effective mechanism for initiating changes in work procedures and methods and/or requesting new or additional resources such as new technology they may feel they need to improve performance and realize gains? While management must control the allocation of resources, gainsharing participants have a right to expect that management will agree to reasonable and justifiable requests for additional resources and/or changes in work methods.		
8.	If the work of multiple groups, departments, or divisions will affect performance measured by the gainsharing formula, is there an effective mechanism for coordinating the efforts of the multiple groups involved and insuring high levels of communication, information sharing, and cooperation?		
9.	Are other social and/or financial reward programs, currently in existence or planned, consistent with the gainsharing program? For example, are managerial and supervisory bonus/incentive programs consistent with the gainsharing plan? Are existing social award and recognition programs such as "employee of the month" or suggestion awards, consistent with the gainsharing plan?		
10.	Does the culture of the group, department, and/or organization as a whole support employee involvement, empowerment, and the participation of employees in decision-making? Will most employees be willing to take some financial risk and accept greater responsibilities in return for financial rewards and greater control over their work life? Will the owners/managers of the business be willing to give up some control over the way work is performed in order to gain greater employee commitment and the benefit of their ideas? Will the owners/managers of the business be willing to share the financial gains that come from employee efforts even if the gainsharing bonuses turn out to be substantial—10%, 20%, or even more?		

Troubleshooting Gainsharing
The 20 Keys to Success

If your gainsharing program is not producing the results you desire, here are some questions to ask that may help you pinpoint where your program went wrong and what you can do to improve.

	QUESTION	YES	NO
1.	Did you build a business case for gainsharing? Did you align the program and rewards with the business strategy? Does gainsharing support your business objectives?		
2.	Did you implement gainsharing in a capital-intensive organization? Gainsharing has been shown to be most successful in labor-intensive organizations where employees can significantly affect performance outcomes thorough their ideas and actions.		
3.	Did you implement gainsharing during a time of financial crisis or when the business did not have the funds to invest in program administration and employee development and training?		
4.	Did you rely to heavily upon outside consultants? Managers and employees must design the gainsharing plan themselves in order to develop a sense of ownership of the plan and to acquire the skills to be able to maintain and revise the plan over time.		
5.	Did you design the plan in isolation without adequate input from managers, supervisors, team leaders, the union and employees?. Gainsharing plans designed by outside consultants or a single or small group of managers without employee and/or union input are doomed to failure.		
6.	Did you spend an adequate amount of time designing the gainsharing plan? You should spend from six to nine months designing the gainsharing plan. It takes that amount of time to work through all of the issues and to gain commitment to the plan. Plans that are designed in haste quickly fail.		
7.	Did you involve the union early on in the gainsharing design process? You must gain union support or at least acquiescence to gainsharing or your plan cannot succeed.		
8.	Did you involve employees in the decision to undertake gainsharing and in the design process? Consider having employees vote on the plan and do not proceed unless 80 percent of employees approve.		
9.	Did you keep the gainsharing participant group relatively small? The number of participants covered by a single gainsharing plan should be less than 500 and preferably less than 200.		
10.	Did you keep the plan simple and easy to understand? Did you the formula contain only items that were controllable by plan participants?		
11.	Were the gainsharing targets reasonable and justifiable given historical trends and competitive requirements? Were the targets seen as fair and reasonable by employees and managers alike?		
12.	Was the potential for gains sufficient to produce average bonus payments of $100 per month per employee? Ideally, employees should have to potential of earning average bonuses of $200 per month or more. Research suggests that it takes bonuses, or at least the potential for bonuses, of $100 per month to get employees' attention and $200 per month to get them excited.		
13.	Did you calculate and pay gainsharing bonuses monthly or weekly rather than quarterly or annually? Employees will see a greater connection between their efforts and gainsharing bonuses if the bonuses are paid close to the time of the performance that led to the gain.		

	QUESTION	YES	NO
14.	Did you attempt to implement gainsharing without strong support from the senior executives of the organization and the majority of managers and supervisors? The senior manager of the organization implementing gainsharing should be prepared to state his/her commitment to the philosophy of gainsharing and the organization's gainsharing plan both verbally and in writing prior to the implementation of the plan.		
15.	Was a structured system of employee involvement such as employee teams or a suggestion system in place and operational BEFORE the start of gainsharing? Were employees and managers fully trained in the operation of the involvement system?		
16.	Did employees understand the drivers of the gainsharing formula and how they could affect the potential for gains by changes in their behavior? There should be a direct "line-of-sight" between employee behavior and gainsharing results.		
17.	Did you invest heavily in employee training and re-training to ensure that employees understood the gainsharing plan and had the problem-solving and other skills necessary to find ways to make gains happen?		
18.	Did you make extensive use of banners, meetings, bulletin boards, newsletters and other communication devices to keep employees informed about the status of the gainsharing program during the design process and once the program was implemented? Did you do an adequate job of communicating with employees about the gainsharing plan and how to make gains happen?		
19.	Did you implement the gainsharing plan when business conditions were good and there was the potential to realize early gains? Did the organization realize early gains? If not, why not?		
20.	Do you conduct regularly scheduled formal reviews of the gainsharing plan (at least annually) to make sure the plan is working for employees, the company and other stakeholders? Have you revise the plan as necessary based upon what you have learned?		

Boyett & Associates

Consultants to Innovative Management
125 Stepping Stone Lane
Alpharetta, GA 30004-4009
770-667-9904
Fax: 770-667-9906

Please contact us if you need additional advice and assistance in designing your gainsharing plan.

Visit our Web Sites at:

http://www.jboyett.com

and

http://www.guruguide.com

0-595-32408-8